D0122606

THE AMERICAN BAR ASSOCIATION

LEGAL GUIDE FOR OLDER AMERICANS

Other Books by the American Bar Association

The American Bar Association Family Legal Guide
The American Bar Association Guide to Home Ownership
The American Bar Association Guide to Wills and Estates
The American Bar Association Guide to Family Law
The American Bar Association Guide to Consumer Law
The American Bar Association Guide to Workplace Law

THE AMERICAN BAR ASSOCIATION

LEGAL GUIDE FOR OLDER AMERICANS

The Law Every American Over Fifty Needs to Know

NATIONAL UNIVERSITY LIBRARY SAN DIEGO

TIMES BOOKS
RANDOM HOUSE

NON CIRCULATING

Points of view or opinions in this publication do not necessarily represent the official policies or positions of the American Bar Association.

The book is not a substitute for an attorney, nor does it attempt to answer all questions about all situations you may encounter.

Copyright © 1998 by the American Bar Association

All rights reserved under International and Pan-American Copyright Conventions. Published in the United States by Times Books, a division of Random House, Inc., New York, and simultaneously in Canada by Random House of Canada, Limited, Toronto.

Random House website address: www.randomhouse.com

Printed in the United States of America on acid-free paper

American Bar Association.
The American Bar Association legal guide for older Americans: the law every American over fifty needs to know / the American Bar Association.
p. cm.
Includes index.
ISBN 0-8129-2937-3 (pbk.)
1. Aged—Legal status, laws, etc.—United States. 2. Aged—Medical care—Law and legislation—United States. 3. Old age assistance—Law and legislation—United States. I. Title.
KF390.A4A43 1997
346.7301'3—dc21 97-22270

9 8 7 6 5 4 3 2

First Edition

AMERICAN BAR ASSOCIATION

Robert A. Stein, *Executive Director*

Sarina A. Butler, *Associate Executive Director, Communications Group*

Mabel C. McKinney-Browning, *Director, Division for Public Education*

Charles White, *Series Editor*

STANDING COMMITTEE ON PUBLIC EDUCATION

Allan J. Tanenbaum, *Chair*

PRINCIPAL AUTHOR

Charles P. Sabatino, *Assistant Director,*
with Nancy Coleman, *Director*, and
Stephanie Edelstein, Naomi Karp, Lori Stiegel, Erica Wood,
Staff Attorneys
Commission on Legal Problems of the Elderly
American Bar Association
Washington, D.C.

REVIEWERS

Karen Ferguson
Pension Rights Center
Washington, D.C.

Gregory French
Pro Seniors, Inc.
Cincinnati, Ohio

Sally Hurme
Legal Counsel for the Elderly
AARP
Washington, D.C.

John J. Lombard, Jr.
Morgan, Lewis & Bockius, LLP
Philadelphia, Pennsylvania

Anne E. Moss
Fierst & Moss
Washington, D.C.

Martha Pelaez
SE Florida Center on Aging
Florida International University
North Miami, Florida

Jeremy Perlin
Staff Director
ABA Committee on Specialization
Chicago, Illinois

John H. Pickering
Former Chairperson
ABA Commission on Legal Problems of the Elderly
Washington, D.C.

W. A. Schneeberg
Attorney at Law
Garland, Texas

Sheree Swetin
Staff Director
ABA Committee on Lawyer Referral
Chicago, Illinois

Robin Talbert
Senior Program Specialist
AARP
Washington, D.C.

Raymond H. Young
Young & Bayle
Boston, Massachusetts

AMERICAN BAR ASSOCIATION

Standing Committee on Public Education

Allan J. Tanenbaum, Chair
Atlanta, Georgia

Antonio Alvarado
Austin, Texas

Berl I. Bernhard
Washington, D.C.

William J. Brennan III
Princeton, New Jersey

N. Kay Bridger-Riley
Tulsa, Oklahoma

Rachelle Bedke Chong
Washington, D.C.

Sally Lee Foley
Bloomfield Hills, Michigan

Kirk G. Forrest
Tulsa, Oklahoma

Vanne Owens Hayes
Minneapolis, Minnesota

Howard M. Kirshbaum
Denver, Colorado

Charles Ogletree
Cambridge, Massachusetts

Gregory A. Vega
San Diego, California

Georgina Verdugo
Washington, D.C.

Howard H. Vogel
Knoxville, Tennessee

Margaret Bush Wilson
St. Louis, Missouri

CONTENTS

FOREWORD

Allan J. Tanenbaum, *Chair*
ABA Standing Committee on Public Education

THIS BOOK IS PART OF A SERIES of handbooks giving the public accurate, up-to-date, and, above all, understandable practical information about the law that impacts everyone, every day. It's a key part of the ABA's public education program, which is designed to help people deal effectively with practical legal matters.

In this book, we focus on the legal needs of the fastest-growing segment of our population—older persons. We've given plenty of ideas on how the law protects the rights of older people to Social Security, Medicare, and other government programs.

We discuss how the law impacts health care, housing, and pension rights, as well as ways to save money and hassle by planning your estate, and ways of assuring that your wishes will be followed in the event that you're incapacitated. We even get into grandparents' rights, the rights of people with disabilities, and the special concerns of older consumers.

But this guide isn't just for older persons. It's of tremendous help to the *families* of older people. They, too, are involved in helping parents (and maybe even grandparents) plan for their later years, and often, in the course of this planning, they begin to think ahead and plan for their own retirement. This book can help these younger people get a head start on checking their Social Security benefits, evaluating their pension options, creating their own estate plans, and otherwise taking the steps to assure that they understand and can use all the protections the law allows.

The authors of this book explain the many legal protections of older Americans clearly and simply. They take out the jargon and fancy words, and put in plenty of tips that will help you in all kinds of everyday transactions. The final section of each chapter gives you contact information about dozens of organizations that can provide free or inexpensive information and assistance, and the last chapter provides an overview of the legal and nonlegal help that's available.

To make this book as useful as possible, the authors define all the key terms in everyday language, use plenty of examples drawn from ordinary life, and accompany the text with short articles highlighting additional points of interest.

Other books in this series may also help. *The ABA Guide to Wills and Estates* gives you practical steps to save time, money, and trouble by planning *now*. *The ABA Guide to Consumer Law* looks at a full range of money-saving legal protections. *The ABA Guide to Workplace Law* gives you tips on laws against age discrimination and other kinds of discrimination, and also helps you understand the legal protections of pensions and other retirement benefits.

Sometimes a problem is so complex, or so much is at stake, that you'll want to seek legal advice from someone who knows the facts of your particular case and can give you advice tailored to your situation. But this book will give you a solid grounding in the law affecting older persons that will help you deal with the myriad circumstances that can affect you and your loved ones.

Allan J. Tanenbaum is a practicing attorney in Atlanta, Georgia, with the law firm of Cohen, Pollock, Merlin, Axelrod & Tanenbaum, where he concentrates in business and tax law issues. He represents the State Bar of Georgia in the ABA House of Delegates.

PREFACE

Robert A. Stein, *Executive Director*
American Bar Association

THE AMERICAN BAR ASSOCIATION legal guides are designed to provide guidance for people on important legal questions they encounter in everyday life. When American families are asked to describe their legal needs, the topics that come up repeatedly are housing, personal finance, family and domestic concerns (usually in conjunction with divorce and child support), wills and estates, and employment-related issues. In addition, more and more Americans have questions about operating a business, often out of the home.

These are the topics that *The American Bar Association Legal Guides* cover in plain, direct language. We have made a special effort to make the books practical, by using situations and problems you are likely to encounter. The goal of these books is to give helpful information on a range of options that can be used in solving everyday legal problems, so that you can make informed decisions on how best to handle your particular question.

The American Bar Association wants Americans to be aware of the full range of options available when they are confronted with a problem that might have a "legal" solution. The Association has supported programs to eliminate delay in the courts, and has worked to promote fast, affordable alternatives to lawsuits, such as mediation, arbitration, conciliation, and small claims court. Through ABA support for lawyer referral programs and pro bono services (where lawyers donate their time), people have been able to find the best lawyer for their particular case and have received quality legal help within their budget.

The American Bar Association Legal Guides discuss all these alternatives, suggesting the wide range of options open to you. We hope that they will help you feel more comfortable with the law and will remove much of the mystery from the legal system.

Several hundred members of the Association have contributed to *The American Bar Association Legal Guides*—as authors and as reviewers who have guaranteed the guides' accuracy. To them—and to the ABA's Standing Committee on Public Education, which was the primary force behind the publications—I express my thanks and gratitude, and that of the Association and of lawyers everywhere.

Robert A. Stein is executive director of the American Bar Association. He was formerly dean of the University of Minnesota Law School.

INTRODUCTION

Charles P. Sabatino,
ABA Commission on Legal Problems of the Elderly

WHY A LEGAL GUIDE for older people and their families? A generation ago, even a few years ago, this book was unnecessary. Now both the law and society have changed. There's a wide array of laws directly addressing the legal needs of older people, and a growing recognition that the law is crucial to the social and health needs of older persons and their families.

The driving force behind this book springs from at least four realities.

- First, we are rapidly aging as a society. Far more people are living to their seventh, eighth, ninth, and tenth decades of life than ever before. Thus, the problems and opportunities of aging affect more older persons and more families of older persons than at any time in history.
- Second, the law permeates almost every aspect of our society, especially the programs, protections, and opportunities that benefit older persons. This book provides a basic knowledge of the law that will help you navigate through programs such as Medicare, Medicaid, Social Security, or pension benefits.
- Third, the personal and financial autonomy of older persons is at greater risk than that of the remainder of the adult population, because of the increasing risk of physical and mental impairment. This book responds to this risk by offering an array of planning strategies to preserve personal autonomy and financial stability.

- Fourth, older persons and their families are more mobile and more diverse than ever before. Caregiving within families frequently takes place over great distances and in a growing variety of home and community-based settings. This book helps you plan for and manage caregiver responsibilities, as well as protect older people in their choice of living arrangements.

The American Bar Association recognized the need to give special attention to issues of law and aging back in 1978 when it established an interdisciplinary Commission on Legal Problems of the Elderly. That commission is busier than ever today advocating for the needs of older persons, educating the professions that serve older persons about the legal rights and responsibilities of this population, and, by virtue of publications such as this guide, educating the general public. If you are an "aging" adult—as we all are—or are concerned with planning for your later years or helping a parent or other relative or friend deal with the problems of aging, then this guide is for you.

THE AMERICAN BAR ASSOCIATION

LEGAL GUIDE FOR OLDER AMERICANS

CHAPTER ONE

Age Discrimination in Employment

PROTECTING THE RIGHTS OF OLDER WORKERS has been a national priority for many years. In the early 1960s, employers commonly discriminated against older workers because of negative stereotypes of aging and faulty assumptions about the costs and productivity of older workers. In response, in 1967, Congress passed the **Age Discrimination in Employment Act (ADEA)**. This federal law attempts to secure fair and equal treatment for workers forty and over by:

- promoting the employment of older persons based on their ability rather than age;
- prohibiting arbitrary age discrimination in employment;
- helping employers and workers find ways of meeting problems arising from the impact of age on employment.

The act is even more important today. Corporate streamlining in the form of **downsizing**—layoffs, production cutbacks, plant closings, corporate mergers, restructurings, and technological change—has become the norm. Older workers are more likely to face discrimination in hiring and layoff policies and sometimes not-so-obvious discrimination in early retirement incentives or severance benefit offers.

The Age Discrimination in Employment Act applies to most, but not all, workers forty and over. The most significant exclusion is of small businesses employing fewer than twenty workers. However, the act does apply to:

1. private employers with twenty or more employees;
2. all state, federal, and local government employers;
3. employment agencies of any size;
4. labor organizations with twenty-five or more members.

Who is protected? The act protects most employees forty and older. Previously, the act's protection stopped at age seventy, but the age cap was removed in 1987. Even if you work in a foreign country, you are protected if you work for an American corporation or its subsidiary and if the ADEA does not directly conflict with the law of the country you work in.

HOW WIDESPREAD IS "DOWNSIZING"?

Nearly a third of all U.S. companies had fewer employees on the payroll in 1995 than they did in 1990, and nearly two-thirds underwent at least one workforce reduction. Annually, the share of companies that has reduced the total number of employees has declined slightly in recent years but remains well over 25 percent.

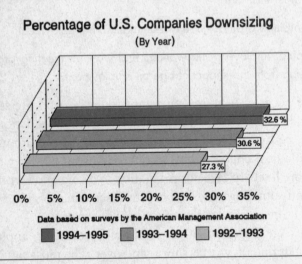

Percentage of U.S. Companies Downsizing
(By Year)

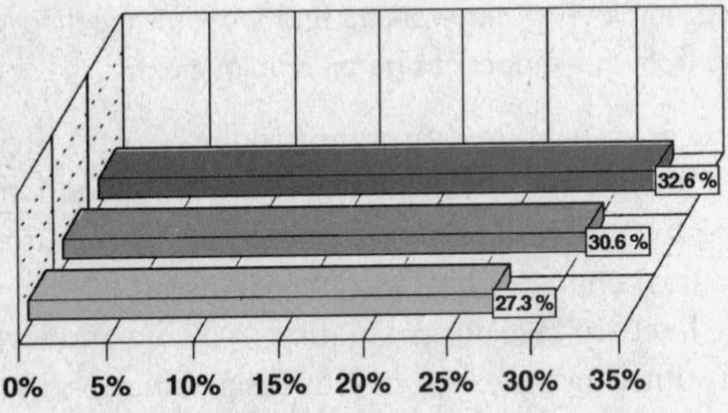

What is prohibited? Generally, the ADEA prohibits:

- discrimination against workers age forty and older in all aspects of employment;
- the use of age preferences in notices or advertisements for employment;
- retaliation against employees for complaining about age discrimination or for helping government investigations of alleged age discrimination.

In addition, labor organizations and employment agencies may not discriminate on the basis of age in membership activities and referrals.

The ADEA prohibits discrimination even within the protected age group (i.e., those forty and older). For example, an employer cannot favor a forty-five-year-old over a sixty-year-old because of age.

Can an employer discriminate against you if your age is only one of several reasons you were discriminated against? As long as age is a **determining factor** for the discrimination, you are protected by the ADEA. Age does not have to be the sole factor. Other unlawful forms of discrimination, based on factors such as race or sex, are covered by other laws.

ADEA's breadth. The ADEA prohibits employers from doing anything that harms your status because of age. This may range all the way from offensive age-related jokes to using age as a factor in hiring, firing, layoff, promotion, demotion, working conditions and hours, training opportunities, compensation, or benefits. Most ADEA lawsuits involve firings or layoffs of older workers.

SOME EXAMPLES OF UNLAWFUL DISCRIMINATION

Mandatory retirement. You simply cannot be forced to retire when you reach a certain age. Nor can your employer penalize you for continuing employment at a certain age by forcing you to take a less responsible job or accept a lower salary.

Like most rules of law, there are exceptions. The act does not apply to elected officials, appointees in policy-making positions, and their immediate advisers. A second exception applies to persons who have been in a "bona fide executive" or "high policy-making" position for at least two years *and* whose retirement benefits (i.e., benefits from pension, profit-sharing plans, savings, or deferred compensation) add up to at least $44,000 a year, not counting Social Security.

Yes, $44,000 is ridiculously low for "executive" compensation by today's standards, but the figure is fixed in the act and is not adjusted yearly. Having a salary over this figure is not enough to fall within the exception. The exception is intended to apply to relatively few top-level employees in an organization who exercise substantial authority over a significant number of employees. If you fall within this group, you may be subject to mandatory retirement at age sixty-five. However, the other discrimination protections of the act described below still apply.

A third exception applies to public safety officers, such as firefighters and police. The act permits their mandatory retirement at any age specified by state or local law, as well as upper age limits on hiring. A similar exception used to apply to tenured faculty employed by universities, but since December 31, 1993, tenured faculty have been protected from mandatory retirement.

Discrimination in hiring—the "overqualified" worker. Discrimination can be hard to detect. However, one common response to older workers with a great deal of experience is that the applicant is "overqualified" or "This job wouldn't suit your qualifications."

Whether this is legal depends on the nature of the job and the surrounding circumstances. Sometimes, it might be reasonable to deny you a job because you have too much experience or education. For example, someone with a Ph.D. in education could be overqualified for a teacher's aide position that requires only two years of college education. In other cases, a court might decide that calling you "overqualified" is just an employer's pretext (excuse) to avoid hiring an older worker. Be wary if a potential employer says, "I'm sure that with your long experience, you wouldn't be interested in this entry-level position."

Layoffs or downsizing by employers. The ADEA prohibits employers from using age as a factor in layoffs or **reductions in force** (downsizing). Employers may make layoff decisions based on reasonable factors other than age, such as on performance evaluations, skill level, or seniority (last hired, first fired). However, sometimes those factors merely mask age discrimination. For example, if an employer lays off only higher-paid employees, the employer may be discriminating unlawfully against older employees. Higher pay is often synonymous with greater age. Whether this is age discrimination depends on the employer's motive.

When a layoff does occur, the act explicitly prohibits an employer from reducing your severance benefits or other layoff benefits just because you are eligible for a pension or pension-related benefit, except in certain narrowly defined circumstances.

Compensation and fringe benefits. Wage discrimination, based on age, is clearly illegal and probably rare. More likely is discrimination in job-related fringe benefits such as insurance. The general rule requires employers to provide all age groups the same benefit, or provide a benefit that costs the same for all age groups. For example, if a life insurance benefit costs the employer more for older workers, then the employer may provide older workers a smaller insurance benefit, as long as the cost of the benefit to the employer is the same as that offered to younger workers.

As to health insurance, employers must cover older workers and their spouses under the same conditions as younger workers. While you are employed, your benefits cannot be lowered just because you become eligible for Medicare. In fact, the employer insurance must remain the primary insurer. Medicare will cover you as a secondary insurer.

Training and promotions. Older workers must be given the same privileges of employment as younger workers. These privileges include training. Employers can't simply say, "Younger workers will be with the company longer."

Likewise, older workers must be given the same chance to receive promotions as all other workers. But age does not *entitle* a person to a promotion; an employer may have a valid reason, apart from age, for promoting a younger person rather than an older one.

Job assignments, demotions, working conditions. Employers cannot force you to take a less responsible job or lower-paying position because of your age. This sometimes occurs subtly when an employer gradually shifts more and more responsibilities from an older worker to others without adequate justification. If working conditions, hours, or other elements in your working environment are changed for the worse, these changes may also violate the ADEA if based on age or the desire to make work so unpleasant that you quit.

Performance evaluation. Performance evaluations must not be age-biased in content or in the way they are applied. Be wary of any job performance system that is applied differently to older workers than to younger workers. A legitimate performance evaluation system should be objective, age neutral in content and the way it is administered, and have "teeth"—

that is, it should have real consequences for your continued employment.

Harassment. All age harassment is illegal. Managers can't harass you because of your age, nor can they permit others to harass you. For example, older workers should not be made to feel uncomfortable because they are too "old-fashioned," "out of synch," or "old dogs" who can't learn new tricks.

Advertising. Advertisements may not exclude or discourage older workers from applying, unless age is a **bona fide occupational qualification (BFOQ).** For example, an age limit would be permissible in advertising for someone to model teen clothing, but not for a clerk job to sell teen clothing. A general rule is that advertisements cannot imply that only certain age groups are wanted for the job.

Retaliation for making an ADEA complaint. Retaliation for making an ADEA charge is illegal. Thus, if your employer directly or indirectly withholds expected resources or work assignments from you, or your working conditions obviously decline, or if you are subjected to a hostile attitude by supervisors, these all violate the ADEA and become additional grounds for another ADEA charge. Because these behaviors can be subtle, keep good notes about particular actions.

Discrimination based on disability. The ADEA protects you only from discrimination based on age. If an illness or disability prevents you from doing your job satisfactorily, the ADEA does not prevent your employer from requiring you to retire, regardless of your age. However, other federal and state laws—including the 1990 **Americans with Disabilities Act (ADA)**—forbid discrimination against persons with disabilities or handicaps, including those associated with certain illnesses. So, if the ADEA does not cover you in these circumstances, you should consider whether you are being unfairly treated because of disability. Your protections under the ADA are described in chapter 6.

EARLY RETIREMENT INCENTIVES

More and more employers are using "early retirement incentives" to reduce their workforces. Common incentives include:

- paying full retirement benefits to workers who retire early;
- supplementing retirement benefits with additional cash ("bridge payments") for a limited period of time to help you until you become eligible for Social Security benefits;
- adding age and/or service credits to your work record to enable you to meet pension eligibility provisions at an earlier age or increasing the benefits you would otherwise receive at your age.

The ADEA permits voluntary early retirement incentive plans such as these that are part of bona fide employee benefit plans and consistent with the purposes of the ADEA. Thus, a simple lump-sum bonus for employees over fifty-five who choose to retire would be acceptable. But if the bonus has an upper age cap, say sixty years old, then the plan would be discriminatory, because a sixty-one-year-old would be denied the benefit being offered to the younger age group.

Early retirement plans can provide substantial benefits if you're willing to retire early. However, giving up employment also has great disadvantages, economically and personally, such as loss of income, loss of regular activity, or loss of professional status. You should be given sufficient information and plenty of time to consider an early retirement offer. Review your options with a financial adviser if possible. You should not receive threats of layoff or demotion if you do not choose early retirement. This kind of pressure, express or implied, raises doubt about whether the plan is truly voluntary.

Waiving your ADEA rights. Some companies ask employees who accept an early retirement offer or other exit incentive to sign a **waiver** of their rights under the ADEA, including the right to sue the employer. Waivers are legal only if they are "knowing and voluntary" and the employer follows specific procedures required by the act, including extensive notice, disclosure of information, and time periods to ensure that employees have sufficient time to make a decision.

SOME ADEA EXCEPTIONS

Certain employer practices are lawful even though they may adversely affect older workers.

Bona fide occupational qualifications. If an employer can prove that age is a "bona fide occupational qualification" (BFOQ), discrimination is allowed. One obvious example of age as a BFOQ is a part in a movie requiring a child actor. However, the BFOQ exception is difficult to prove, and the burden of proof is on the employer. The employer must show: first, that the job qualifications are reasonably necessary to the essence of the employer's business; and second, that substantially all persons over the age limit cannot perform the job safely and efficiently, or that it is impossible or highly impractical to assess fitness on an individualized basis.

Reasonable factors other than age. This is a commonsense exception. Employers may base decisions about hiring, firing, or other actions on reasonable factors other than age, if justified by business necessity. A simple example is using performance evaluations and physical exams, which are perfectly acceptable as long as the factors are applied fairly to workers of all ages. In every case, reasonable factors other than age must be related to the job, and the factor *cannot* include age.

Good cause. Another commonsense exception, **good cause** usually refers to poor job performance. A discharge for tardiness or proven deficiencies in performance constitutes a "good cause" discharge.

Seniority systems. An employer may observe the terms of a bona fide seniority system. Seniority systems seldom cause a problem under the ADEA, since they normally favor long-term workers over those with shorter tenure.

ENFORCING YOUR ADEA RIGHTS

There are two possible steps you can take. The first is to file a complaint with the state or federal agency responsible for enforcing the ADEA. The second is to file a lawsuit, usually in federal court.

STEP 1—FILING A CHARGE

If you have been forced to retire, fired, or otherwise discriminated against because of your age, you should file a charge of age discrimination in writing with the federal **Equal Employment Opportunity Commission (EEOC).** The EEOC is the federal agency with the power to investigate, mediate, and file lawsuits to end age discrimination, as well as discrimination based on race, sex, disability, and other grounds.

If your state has an age discrimination law and enforcement agency (not every state has one), you may file the complaint with the state agency. To be on the safe side, it is a good idea to file with both the EEOC and the state agency. It is important to check the applicable laws in your state. Some state statutes offer more protection against discrimination than the ADEA. If you are unsure whether your state has an enforcement agency, contact your state's department of labor or an EEOC office in your area.

If you file a **charge,** your name will be disclosed to the employer. If you wish to remain anonymous, you can file a **complaint** instead. A complaint should trigger an EEOC investigation; however, the government gives complaints lower priority than charges. In addition, even if EEOC action leads an employer to correct its discriminatory practices, your own past unfair treatment may not be remedied if you filed only a complaint.

You should include as much relevant data as possible when you file a charge. Be sure to include information about how to contact you, the name and address of the discriminating party, the type of discrimination, relevant dates and witnesses, and specific facts. If pertinent, you might also include employment contracts, brochures, or similar documents that demonstrate company policy. Before you file the charge, make sure you sign it.

Be aware of time limits! Normally, you have 180 days from the date of the violation or reasonable notice of it (whichever occurs first). If you are given notice of layoff on January 1, to take effect March 1, the time limit begins to run from the earlier date when you received notice and not the date of layoff.

If your state has an age discrimination law and enforcement agency, the time limit may be extended to 300 days, but make every effort to act within the 180 days to be on the safe side.

Once you file a charge with the EEOC or your state agency, the agency is required to contact the discriminating party and attempt conciliation between the parties. If the problem is resolved to everyone's satisfaction at this point, the case is closed. If not, either you or the EEOC can proceed to the next step by filing an age discrimination lawsuit.

While the EEOC has the power to file a lawsuit to enforce your rights, it does so in only a small proportion of cases. The EEOC does not make any formal findings of guilt or innocence on your charge. Only a court can do that.

STEP 2—FILING A PRIVATE LAWSUIT

Before you can file an age discrimination lawsuit in federal or state court, you must have filed a charge with the EEOC as described above. After sixty or more days from the date you filed the charge, you have a right to file a lawsuit under the ADEA, if the EEOC has not filed a lawsuit on your behalf (it seldom does). You do not have to wait for a **right-to-sue notice** from the EEOC. Your own lawsuit will be a private one, and you must bear the court costs and attorney fees. A big advantage of an EEOC suit on your behalf is that you would not be required to pay its costs. If the EEOC files a suit either on its own or on your behalf *before* you do, the commission enforces your rights and you can no longer file a private lawsuit.

Again, *be aware of time limits!* There is a limit to how long you can wait before suing an employer for discrimination. The federal statute of limitations is two years from the time you knew or should have known of the violation. If the violation was willful, you have three years to file a lawsuit.

If there is already a lawsuit against your employer for age discrimination, you may be able to join it. The ADEA allows **class-action lawsuits.** However, unlike in many other class-action cases, you are not automatically part of the subject class just because the alleged discrimination affects you. You must opt in by consenting in writing.

DECIDING WHETHER TO SUE

If you have suffered significant loss as a result of age discrimination and you are willing to invest substantial time and money, filing a private lawsuit may be worthwhile. But weigh the costs of such a lawsuit realistically. ADEA cases can involve a great deal of legal analysis, effort, and **discovery** (the disclosure of documents and information between the parties before trial). Generally, attorneys do not take ADEA cases on a **contingency** basis (that is, payment when and if the case is decided favorably). However, if your lawsuit is successful, the ADEA permits you to seek attorneys' fees and costs from the discriminating party.

The ADEA entitles all litigants under the act to a trial by jury on any issue of fact. If you want a jury trial, you must ask for one specifically. If not, a jury trial is automatically waived.

If you win your case, the court will order the employer to pay damages or provide other remedies to make up to you what you lost through discrimination. This might include:

- awarding back pay for salary you did not receive while unemployed;
- awarding future pay or "front pay" for a period of time (not all courts have been willing to recognize this);
- paying lost benefits, or reinstatement of lost benefits—such as seniority rights, health or insurance benefits, sick leave, savings plan benefits, expected raises, stock bonus plan benefits, and lost overtime pay;
- reinstating your former job, with your former salary and benefits;
- paying double damages in cases of willful violations of the ADEA.

If you win your case, the company that discriminated against you usually will have to pay for your lawyer and other expenses, as well as for court costs.

WHERE TO GET MORE INFORMATION AND HELP

- **Equal Employment Opportunity Commission (EEOC)** offices are listed in the telephone directory under "United States Government." You may also find the location of the office nearest you by calling the EEOC nationwide toll-free number: (800) 669-4000.
- *Laws Enforced by the EEOC* is a general information booklet produced by the EEOC, available at no charge. Call the EEOC toll-free publication number: (800) 669-3362.

- *Age Discrimination on the Job* is a free booklet written by the **American Association of Retired Persons (AARP)** through its Work Force Programs Department (Pub. No. D12386). Available from AARP Fulfillment, 601 E Street, NW, Washington, DC 20049. AARP's home page on the World Wide Web is http://www.aarp.org.

CHAPTER TWO

Retirement Income Rights and Benefits

WHEN YOU RETIRE, your financial security will probably depend on pension income, Social Security benefits, and personal savings. For people without significant income or assets, the federal Supplemental Security Income program and other public benefit programs such as veterans' benefits and federal or state housing subsidy programs may kick in.

One important change in today's work world is that retirement is no longer a well-defined or fixed point in time. More people are choosing to continue working full- or part-time well into their seventies and eighties. Nevertheless, you have to be "retired" or disabled before you're eligible for most pensions and most of the other programs we'll discuss in this chapter.

We begin with an overview of private pensions, followed by Social Security benefits and Supplemental Security Income (SSI). After describing some tax breaks for seniors, the chapter ends with a list of resources that will supply additional information.

PRIVATE PENSIONS

About half the employees working for private companies are covered by private retirement plans. Typically, plans are set up by a company or by an agreement between a labor union and one or more employers. The several types of retirement plans include pension plans, profit-sharing plans, "401(k)" savings plans (sometimes known as thrift plans), and employee stock ownership plans.

Private pension plans must meet minimum standards established by federal laws. The most important law protecting pension rights is the **Employee Retirement Income Security Act of 1974 (ERISA).** ERISA covers most company-sponsored and union-sponsored pension plans. But ERISA does not cover plans sponsored by the federal, state, and local governments, religious entities, or the military. Each of these has its own rules.

Coverage. Employers are not required to provide you with a pension, and even if they do offer a pension, they need not provide pensions for all their workers. Up to 30 percent of an employer's workforce may be excluded. And certain categories of employees may be excluded—for example, secretarial staff and hourly workers. However, with at least 70 percent of the workforce covered, employer pensions cannot just cover the higher-ups in the organization, and it is illegal to discriminate in favor of higher-paid workers.

Employers may set some minimum requirements before an employee's work begins to count toward earning a pension. As a new employee, you may be required to complete one year of service, or reach the age of twenty-one, or both, before being eligible to participate. And companies can require employees to work at least one thousand hours per year (considered half-time) to be part of the plan.

Vesting. Pension plans usually require you to work a specified number of years to earn the right to receive a pension at retirement age. Once you have worked the required length of time, your employer's contributions to your pension **vest**, meaning that you will have a right to collect them. Until your pension vests, you can **accrue** benefits in each year you are a member of the plan, but you won't eventually **collect** them unless you also work long enough to vest.

Once benefits vest, they cannot be taken away, even if you stop working or leave your job before retirement age. On the other hand, if you leave your job before your benefits vest, you lose the contributions made by your employer. If you also contribute to your pension plan from your own salary, your contributions always vest immediately, even if you haven't worked long enough to vest in contributions made by your employer.

Under ERISA's vesting rules, most pension benefits vest fully after five years of service. Employers are also allowed to have what's called a graduated vesting schedule, where part of the benefits vest after you have worked three years, with an increasing portion vesting in years four, five, and six. Full vesting occurs by year seven under this schedule.

HOW VESTING WORKS

Let's look at the work history of Nancy Smith. Nancy worked from 1955 to 1976 for Acme Department Stores. Acme required ten years for her pension to vest (which was permitted back then). From 1977 to 1989, Nancy was employed by Zenith Food Warehouse. Then she went to Pinnacle Designs, from 1990 to 1994. Under Pinnacle's partial vesting scheme, after four years of service, an employee is entitled to a pension equivalent to a percentage of the full pension that vests after seven years. Nancy then worked two days a week for Nadir, Inc., for a year until her retirement in 1995.

Nancy would be entitled to: a pension from Acme based on her twenty-one years of service; a pension from Zenith based on her twelve years there; and a pension from Pinnacle based on their graduated vesting schedule. She would not be entitled to a pension from Nadir, because she didn't work there at least half-time—her two days a week amounted to less than one thousand hours a year, the half-time benchmark. She would start collecting all of these pensions at her retirement in 1995 if she had attained the retirement age specified in these pension plans.

You may be entitled to collect several pensions, as long as you worked in each of a series of jobs long enough for pension benefits to vest.

Retirement age. Pension plans set a **"normal" retirement age** at which vested employees become eligible to collect a full pension without any reduction for age. Normal retirement age is generally sixty-five. However, most plans allow employees to retire earlier—for example, by fifty-five or sixty—with reduced benefits or full benefits, depending on the number of years worked.

Today, older employees completely vest at normal retirement age, regardless of the number of years they have worked for an employer. If you begin working for an employer at sixty-two and normal retirement age is sixty-five, you can retire at sixty-five and still collect a pension.

TYPES OF PENSION PLANS

There are two major kinds of pension plans. Under the traditional **defined benefit plan,** the employer promises you a specific benefit at retirement, based on a formula that generally considers length of service and amount of earnings. Often these plans result from bargaining with unions. A common formula calculates your years of service to pay you a percentage of the average of your last three (or maybe five) years' salary. For example, if you got two percentage points for each year of service and worked thirty-three years, you'd be entitled to 66 percent of your average salary over your last three years.

One advantage of defined benefit plans is that a set level of benefits is guaranteed, and the employer bears the risk if the pension fund's investments do poorly. If the plan goes broke, most benefit amounts are insured up to certain limits by the **Pension Benefit Guaranty Corporation (PBGC).**

In a **defined contribution pension plan,** money is contributed to your individual account. Often the employer contributes a set percentage of your earnings, and you are able to contribute additional funds to the account. Upon retirement, benefits are based upon the total amount contributed, plus any earnings the account has accumulated. Thus, benefits vary depending on how the money is invested. These defined contribution plans are not insured by the PBGC, and you bear substantial risks.

A **401(k) plan** is a particular kind of "do it yourself" defined contribution retirement plan sponsored by employers. It's primarily a tax shelter for your retirement saving. You make contributions, which the employer may match up to a certain amount or according to a schedule set up by the employer.

DISTRIBUTION OF BENEFITS UPON RETIREMENT, DEATH, OR DIVORCE

Several forms of payment are available once you retire. Pension plans ordinarily provide a monthly pension for the rest of your life. Some plans let you choose a one-time lump sum payment, and many retirement plans, such as 401(k)s, pay lump sums soon after you leave the job. If you receive a lump sum, it could cost you a lot in income taxes. But you may be able to roll over your lump sum into an **individual retirement account (IRA)** without tax consequences.

If you are married, the basic payment from a pension plan is a **joint and survivor annuity**. Under this payout plan, your monthly benefit is reduced to leave something for your spouse. When you die, your spouse receives a reduced benefit for the rest of his or her life. Under federal law, your spouse's pension must usually be equal to at least 50 percent of the reduced pension you were collecting. The exact reduction in your pension varies from plan to plan. You cannot sign away the right of your spouse to receive a survivor annuity without your spouse's written consent.

The rules are different for profit-sharing plans and 401(k)s.

Ordinarily, your spouse will get 100 percent of the account balance if you die while working under the plan, unless both of you agree to give up this protection. But during your lifetime, you may withdraw funds in a lump sum without your spouse's knowledge or consent. Similarly, when you leave the job, you can withdraw the funds in a lump sum.

If you are divorced, you may be entitled to a share of your former spouse's pension. The pension rights of divorced spouses are governed by state law and must be awarded by a state court through a **qualified domestic relations order (QDRO).** You may be able to begin collecting your benefit after your spouse retires, after he or she dies, or, in some cases, before your spouse retires if he or she could have started collecting a pension.

KNOW YOUR RIGHTS UNDER YOUR PLAN

ERISA requires your employer to give you detailed information about your plan, including a **summary plan description** (a booklet that summarizes the plan rules, explains how benefits are figured, and tells you when you can collect) and a **financial summary** based on the **full annual financial report** that the law requires be filed regularly with the government. The financial summary helps you analyze whether your pension plan is financially sound and being managed prudently. You also have a right to your **individual benefit statement,** which tells you whether you are vested and the level of benefits you have accrued so far. Many plans give these statements to employees automatically each year. If your company does not, you can request an individual benefit statement once every twelve months.

Your pension plan administrator should be able to provide these documents. If you make a written request for documents, the plan administrator must respond within thirty days.

The summary plan description and financial reports are also available from the Pension and Welfare Benefits Administration, Public Disclosure Room, U.S. Department of Labor, 200 Constitution Avenue, NW, Washington, DC 20210. Be sure to give the exact name of your plan and your employer's federal ID number (found on your W-2 form).

Plans in trouble. A company can close down a pension plan at any time if the plan has serious financial difficulties. If a plan is terminated, and does not have enough money to pay promised benefits, a worker's *defined benefit* pension is likely to be insured by the PBGC. Defined contribution and some other types of plans are not covered by the PBGC. Some benefits are not covered, such as certain disability pension benefits and some early retirement benefits. So if your plan fails, the safety net has lots of holes in it. Your summary plan description will tell you whether your benefits are covered by the PBGC.

Plans not in trouble. Sometimes, an employer will terminate a pension plan for other business reasons. If so, your plan administrator will send you a notice explaining the termination, the amount of pension benefit you have accrued, and payment options. Plans usually will purchase an annuity for you from an insurance company. The PBGC does not guarantee pensions that are paid off through an annuity after a solvent pension plan is terminated.

Pensions and Social Security. Social Security payments may affect your pension benefits. Under some plans, benefits decrease depending on how much you receive from Social Security. This is called "integration of benefits." Check with your plan's administrator. Under federal law, plans that take Social Security payments into account when calculating pension benefits must leave you with at least half your pension. But the law applies only to years worked after 1988. For earlier years, your plan rules could leave you with no benefit after considering your Social Security.

CLAIMING YOUR PENSION

Each plan establishes the procedure for submitting pension claims. Each plan also must have an appeals process you can use if you are not satisfied with the plan's action on your claim. Your plan summary should inform you of the filing procedure and appeals process. If your claim is denied, the plan must give you written notice of the decision and state specific reasons for the denial. Then you may file a written appeal with the plan administrator. Be sure to submit all relevant information and documentation at this point—for example, years worked, hours, dates of breaks in service. You may not get another opportunity to submit evidence. The plan should review your appeal promptly and notify you of the result. You have the right to sue in court if you still believe you have been denied benefits unfairly. It is to your definite advantage to retain an attorney specializing in this area of law.

If you think you are entitled to a pension from an old job but you can no longer find the company, the Pension Benefit Guaranty Corporation may be able to help you, especially if the plan was terminated.

SOCIAL SECURITY

The **Social Security Administration (SSA)** administers the country's most extensive programs providing economic security for older and disabled people and their families. Monthly cash benefits include payments to:

- retired workers who have reached at least age sixty-two;
- spouses and dependents of retired workers;
- divorced spouses of retired or disabled workers;
- workers who become disabled;

- spouses and dependents of disabled workers;
- survivors of deceased workers;
- divorced spouses of deceased workers.

All the above benefits are described on the following pages.

Over 95 percent of American workers are eligible for some form of Social Security benefits, including household help, farmworkers, self-employed persons, most employees of state and local government, and some federal workers. Benefits are payable to U.S. citizens and only certain categories of non-citizens. Railroad workers are covered by a separate federal program, **Railroad Retirement,** which is integrated with Social Security.

Social Security programs are complicated, and the laws and regulations governing them change from time to time. Contact your local SSA office for information about Social Security benefits or to ask specific questions about your own case. Offices are listed in the "United States Government" section of your telephone directory. Or call SSA's national toll-free number (800) 772-1213.

QUALIFYING FOR BENEFITS

To be eligible to collect Social Security, you must meet two qualifications. One, you or the worker on whose account the benefits are paid must be "insured" under Social Security. The simplest rule of thumb is that forty quarters of work (ten years) in covered employment will fully insure a worker for life. However, there are many exceptions to this rule. Don't assume you are not covered just because you have fewer than ten years of covered work. Two, you must meet requirements for the particular benefit (that is, be the appropriate age, or be able to prove disability, or dependence on an insured worker, or be the survivor of a deceased worker).

Number of Social Security Beneficiaries
(By Type of Benefit, June 1997)

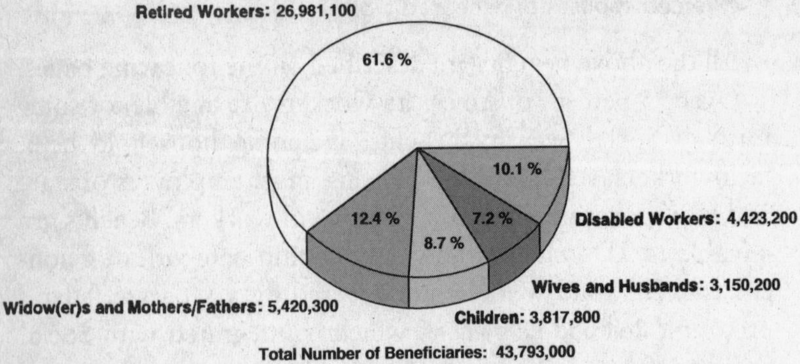

RETIREMENT BENEFITS

Payment levels. Social Security benefits provide only a floor of protection. You will need other sources of income, such as a pension or income from savings, to maintain your style of living. If Social Security is your only income, look into eligibility for Supplemental Security Income or veterans' benefits, described later in this chapter.

The amount you receive from Social Security depends upon how much money you have earned over your lifetime, your age at retirement, and other factors. Any time before retirement, even years before, you can get an estimate of your benefit, called a **Personal Earnings and Benefit Statement.** Just pick up a **Personal Earnings and Benefit Statement Form** from your local SSA office or call the SSA, toll-free, at (800) 772-1213. Or you can file your request through Social Security's home page on the Internet, which is at http://www.ssa.gov. The statement also tells you how much you have paid into the Social Security system. Request this statement every few years to make sure your employers have been reporting your earnings correctly.

Once your benefits begin, you will receive annual cost-of-living adjustments at the start of each calendar year.

Retirement age. Social Security presently considers the **normal retirement age** to be sixty-five. That is the age at which you will receive the normal retirement benefit. If you choose to retire before you reach sixty-five, your benefits will be reduced. The earliest age at which you can receive retirement benefits is sixty-two. If you are fully insured at sixty-two, you will receive approximately 80 percent of your full benefit amount, and you will continue to receive reduced benefits even after you turn sixty-five. If you retire between sixty-two and sixty-five, your benefits are reduced, but the reduction is less. Conversely, if you choose *not* to retire at the normal retirement age, you earn **delayed retirement credits** for each month you continue to work without receiving retirement benefits, and your monthly benefits will be higher when you do decide to receive them.

If you were born in 1938 or later, the normal retirement age will be raised for you. Between 2000 and 2025, normal retirement age under Social Security will be pushed up in small steps until 2025, when the normal retirement age will become sixty-seven. The option of early retirement at age sixty-two will still be available, but the amount of the early retirement benefit will shrink.

WHAT IF MY WAGES WERE WRONGLY REPORTED?

You have approximately three years from the year the wages were earned to correct most mistakes in your earnings record. However, there is no time limit on correcting an error caused by an employer's failure to report your earnings. You can fix these mistakes anytime, but you will need proof. A pay stub or a written statement from the employer will do the trick. You will need to obtain form **OAR-7008 (Request for Correction of Earnings Record)** from the Social Security Administration.

Effect of other income on Social Security retirement. What happens if you work part-time after retirement? If you are under seventy and receiving benefits as a retiree, dependent, or survivor, you may earn only a certain amount of wages before your Social Security retirement benefits are reduced. Under the **retirement earnings test,** the amount you can earn varies depending upon your age:

- **Between sixty-two and sixty-four,** the annual earnings test exempt amount for 1997 is $8,640. If your income exceeds this amount, you lose one dollar of benefits for every two dollars you earn above the cutoff point.

  If you are sixty-four and earn only $8,000 in wages in 1997 and are entitled to Social Security retirement benefits of $10,000, your actual benefit will not be reduced. However, if instead you earned $15,000 in 1997, you would exceed the retirement earnings test by $6,360, resulting in a reduction of your Social Security benefit by $3,180 (i.e., $1 for every $2 of excess earnings). Thus, your reduced benefit for the year would be $6,820.

- **Between the ages of sixty-five and sixty-nine,** the annual earnings test exempt amount for 1997 is $13,500. If your income exceeds this amount, then you lose $1 of benefits for every $3 you earn above the cutoff point.

- **If you are age seventy or older, there is no retirement test.** You may earn an unlimited amount and still receive your full retirement benefit.

The retirement earnings test applies only to **earned income,** defined as gross income from wages or net income from self-employment. Your benefits generally will not be affected by **unearned income**—money earned from savings, investments, insurance, and the like, though they may be reduced if you receive a federal, state, or local government pension.

DISABILITY BENEFITS

Social Security protects all workers under age sixty-five against loss of earnings due to disability. However, you must meet requirements for the number of years employed, age, and the severity of your disability.

Definition of disability. The Social Security Administration defines disability as: (1) The inability to engage in substantial gainful activity (work), (2) because of a medically determinable physical or mental impairment, (3) which can be expected to result in death, or which has lasted or can be expected to last for at least twelve months. All three conditions must be met. The disability must be medically certified, and the guidelines are very strict.

Once you qualify for disability benefits, payments will continue for as long as you remain medically disabled and unable to work. Your health will be reviewed periodically to determine your ability to return to work.

FAMILY BENEFITS

Certain other people *may* receive benefits based on a wage earner's eligibility for retirement or disability benefits. They include the spouse, divorced spouse, and dependents of the insured worker. The benefits described here presume that the worker is still living.

Spouse's benefits. To be eligible to receive benefits, a **current spouse** must:

1. have been married to the worker for at least one year at the time the application is filed

   or

   the couple must be the natural parents of a child

   and

2. be age sixty-two or older

or

be caring for a child who is also eligible to receive benefits on the worker's account (either a minor or a disabled child).

In addition, the worker must be eligible for, though not necessarily receiving, retirement or disability benefits. Thus, a sixty-two-year-old spouse married to a sixty-year-old worker would not be entitled to spouse's benefits until the worker reached age sixty-two. The amount of the spouse's benefit is based upon a percentage of the worker spouse's benefit. At age sixty-five, a spouse collects one-half of what the insured worker would receive. Benefits are reduced further if they begin before the spouse reaches age sixty-five, or if the spouse has extra income under the retirement test or, in some cases, is collecting a government pension. However, a spouse who starts to collect benefits before age sixty-five, but who is also caring for a dependent child, would receive the full spouse's share.

Divorced spouse's benefits. To be eligible to receive benefits, a ***divorced* spouse** must:

1. be at least age sixty-two;
2. have been previously married to the insured worker for at least ten years; and
3. be unmarried.

In addition, the insured worker must be entitled to retirement or disability benefits, *or* if the divorce took place *more than two years ago,* the worker need not be receiving retirement or disability benefits. As long as the worker is at least age sixty-two and fully insured, the divorced spouse may receive benefits.

More than one spouse or divorced spouse can collect on the account of the same retired or disabled worker without affecting the amount received by either the spouse(s) or the worker. A spouse or divorced spouse who is also entitled to benefits on his or her own work record cannot draw both worker and spouse benefits in full, but will receive the higher of the two benefits.

Dependent children's benefits. Social Security makes a distinction between disabled and nondisabled children. Both groups receive benefits equal to approximately one-half of the worker's benefits while the worker is still living, 75 percent if the worker is deceased.

To be eligible to receive benefits, a dependent nondisabled child must:

1. be unmarried and
2. be under eighteen years old

or

be under nineteen if attending elementary or secondary school full-time.

A dependent, **disabled** child of any age may receive benefits *if* the disability begins before the child reaches age twenty-two.

Maximum family benefits. There is a limit on the amount one family can receive in total benefits. The maximum is determined under a formula based on the worker's year of becoming eligible and the size of the worker's primary insurance amount.

SURVIVOR'S BENEFITS

When an insured worker dies, these family members may qualify for survivor's benefits:

- **Spouse** who is at least sixty years old
- **Disabled spouse** who is fifty to fifty-nine years old
- **Divorced spouse** who is at least sixty years old, or fifty if disabled, if the marriage lasted at least ten years

- **Dependent children** who are under eighteen (or under nineteen if attending elementary or high school full-time) or who are disabled
- **Spouse or divorced spouse** of any age caring for a child who is under age sixteen or disabled (called mother's or father's benefits)
- **Parents** who are sixty-two or older and who received at least half of their support from the worker at the time of his or her death

DEATH BENEFITS

When an insured worker dies, Social Security pays a one-time, lump sum death benefit of $255 to only one of the following in the order of priority listed:

- the surviving spouse living with the worker at the time of death; or
- the surviving spouse not living with the deceased worker, but eligible for survivor's benefits in the month of the worker's death; or
- a surviving child eligible for dependent's benefits in the month of the worker's death.

If a person receiving Social Security benefits dies, the check for the month in which the person dies must be returned to SSA.

TERMINATION OF BENEFITS

Disability benefits may be terminated if you recover or refuse to accept rehabilitation services. **Retirement or survivor's benefits** may be terminated if:

- you leave the United States for more than six months;
- you are deported;

- you are convicted of certain crimes, such as treason and espionage; or
- you are in prison, convicted of a felony.

In addition, persons receiving benefits as a widow/widower, divorced spouse, mother/father of a dependent or disabled person, or a parent of a worker may lose their benefit upon remarriage. However, there are many exceptions to this rule. Review your circumstances with an SSA claims representative.

If changes in your circumstances cause a reduction or termination of your benefits, you must receive a letter notifying you of the change. You have the right to appeal.

TAXES ON BENEFITS

Every January, the Social Security Administration sends beneficiaries a **Social Security Benefit Statement**, which includes the benefits received during the previous year. Social Security benefits are not generally taxable. However, people with substantial incomes from other sources plus Social Security may have to pay taxes on part of their benefits. See IRS Publication 915, *Social Security and Equivalent Railroad Retirement Benefits.*

APPLYING FOR BENEFITS

If you are retiring, file two or three months before your retirement date. Applications take this long to process. Your first check should arrive soon after you quit working. Don't delay filing for either retirement or survivor's benefits because you will get paid retroactive benefits only for the six months prior to the month you file your application.

For disability benefits, apply as soon as you realize that you can no longer work. Disability applications can take much longer to process. You can get up to twelve months' retroactive benefits for disability.

When you apply for **retirement benefits,** you should bring:

- your Social Security card or proof of the number;
- a birth certificate or other proof of age;
- W-2 forms from the past two years or, if you are self-employed, copies of your last two federal income tax returns;
- if applicable, proof of military service, since you may be able to receive extra credit for active military duty.

When you apply for **survivor's benefits,** you should bring:

- a copy of the deceased worker's death certificate, and
- proof of your relationship:
  - for a spouse—a marriage certificate, and if claiming as a divorced spouse, a divorce decree;
  - for a dependent child—a birth certificate and evidence of financial dependence;
  - for dependent parents—evidence of financial dependence.

If you are applying for **benefits based on disability,** you should also bring:

- a list, with addresses and telephone numbers, of the doctors, hospitals, or institutions that have treated you for your disability;
- a summary of all the jobs you have held for the past fifteen years and the type of work you performed; and
- information about any other checks you receive for your disability.

SSA DECISIONS AND APPEALS

When you deal with the Social Security Administration, avoid delays and complications by keeping a full, organized account of your communications. Make a note of when you had each conversation, who you spoke with, and what was said. When you file a claim, you are automatically assigned a SSA worker. Keep this person's name and telephone number handy in case you need to contact the SSA.

Be sure you keep copies of forms or documents for yourself. Since the SSA files records by Social Security number, put your Social Security number on the top of each page you submit.

If your claim is approved, you will be told how much your benefits will be and when to expect your first check. If your claim is denied, your letter should list the reasons. You have the right to appeal the Social Security Administration's decision in your case. You have sixty days from the date of notification to appeal. Be sure to get a written denial; you cannot appeal an oral statement.

Since many claim decisions are reversed on appeal, it is usually worth your time and effort to appeal. Also, if you do not appeal, the claim decision becomes final and you give up the chance to appeal later.

Each step in the appeal process results in a decision. If the decision is unfavorable, you have the right to move to the next step, generally within sixty days of receiving a written notice of the decision. SSA measures this deadline by counting sixty-five days from the date posted on the determination letter from SSA.

Step 1—Reconsideration. The first step is to file a written **request for reconsideration** of your claim. An SSA employee other than the one who first decided your claim will examine your file to see whether the decision should be changed. You may add more documents to your file.

You should receive written notice of the reconsideration decision within thirty days. However, reconsideration in disability claims will take longer, usually two or three months.

Step 2—Hearing. If you still are not satisfied, you may file a written **request for an administrative hearing.** You have sixty days to make such a request. Normally, however, the hearing will not take place for several months.

An impartial administrative law judge of the SSA's Office of Hearings and Appeals will preside over your case. The hearing will be a new examination of your case.

Before the hearing, examine your file to make sure it contains every document you have filed. If your case involves disability, you should provide evidence, such as documents or witnesses, about your medical condition and explain why you cannot work.

At the hearing, you can represent yourself or be represented by a lawyer or nonlawyer advocate. Many attorneys who take Social Security disability cases do so on a contingency basis. If the attorney is successful, he or she is generally limited to a fee of 25 percent of the back benefits.

The judge will send you a written decision on your case, usually within a few months. If your claim is approved, you will normally collect benefits dating back to when you filed your original claim, or farther back if you are entitled to retroactive benefits.

Step 3—Appeals Council. If you disagree with the judge's decision, you may file a written appeal within sixty days with the SSA Appeals Council in Washington, D.C. You do not appear before the Appeals Council, but you can add additional information to your file.

Step 4—Federal Court. If you wish to appeal the decision further, you must sue the SSA in federal district court. From there, you can appeal to the United States Court of Appeals, and, in rare cases, to the United States Supreme Court. Going to court can be expensive. Take into account expenses, the amount of benefits you are claiming, and your chances of winning. Although you are not required to have a lawyer, it's usually recommended that you do. Lawyers generally take these cases on a contingency basis, usually 25 percent of any lump sum recovery.

OVERPAYMENTS

Sometimes, SSA pays benefits incorrectly. If you receive a notice that you have been overpaid, you can file a written **request for reconsideration,** saying that the overpayment did not occur or that the amount of the overpayment was wrongly calculated.

At the same time, you can request that the overpayment be **waived.** This is important if the overpayment was not your fault or it would be a hardship to repay. If you file for the waiver within thirty days, the money will not be taken out of checks until a final decision is reached. You will be asked to fill out an **Overpayment Recovery Questionnaire** that will ask you about the cause of the overpayment and your ability to repay it.

YOUR SOCIAL SECURITY CHECK

Social Security checks normally are mailed the first day of each month and received on the third. The check you receive that day is your benefit for the month *just completed.* You may arrange with SSA to have your checks deposited directly in your bank. This is safe and convenient, and will eventually be mandatory for all federal benefits.

If you are unable to manage your benefits due to disability, Social Security will appoint a **representative payee**—a friend, relative, or even a staff person or volunteer from a local agency—to receive the checks and pay the bills. Even if a family member has authority to handle your finances under a durable power of attorney, SSA generally won't permit that person to endorse your Social Security checks unless he or she has been appointed representative payee. A form to file for representative payee is available from any Social Security office.

SUPPLEMENTAL SECURITY INCOME

The **Supplemental Security Income (SSI)** program pays monthly benefits to people who are:

- sixty-five or older, or disabled, or blind, *and*
- have very limited income and personal property.

The SSI program is run by the Social Security Administration, but you do not need to have a work history under Social Security to qualify for benefits. The disability criteria are the same as that for Social Security disability discussed earlier.

SSI benefits are not large and the eligibility requirements are strict. You must have very little income and own very little property. The federal eligibility rules permit up to $2,000 in countable assets for one person or $3,000 for a couple. These resource maximums are not adjusted yearly. However, SSI considers the following assets exempt and does not count them for purposes of eligibility:

- Your home
- Household goods and personal effects up to $2,000, and wedding rings
- Fair market value of a car (up to $4,500, or no limit if needed for employment or medical appointments)
- Cash value of life insurance, if the face value is less than $1,500; if the face value is higher, the extra cash value is counted as an asset
- Trade/business property needed for self-support (e.g., tools, machinery)
- Value of burial plot
- Up to $1,500 in a burial expense fund (this is simply any account earmarked for burial expenses)

In 1997, SSI paid a maximum monthly benefit of $484 to a single person who had no other income. The maximum monthly benefit for couples was $726. These figures are adjusted each January for cost-of-living increases. Many states supplement SSI benefits in amounts ranging from $15 to more than $150 per month.

It is quite typical for those on SSI to receive Social Security benefits at the same time. In addition, if you receive even $1 per month in SSI benefits, in most states you will be eligible for free medical care through Medicaid.

If you think you may qualify, check with your local Social Security Administration office. You will need to prove your age, and you will need a great deal of information about your financial situation. If you are applying because of disability or blindness, you will also need copies of your medical records.

If you are denied, you can appeal. The appeals process is similar to the process for appealing a Social Security claim.

VETERANS' BENEFITS

The United States Department of Veterans Affairs (DVA) administers several benefits programs for veterans and their families. Veterans' benefits include monthly compensation, pensions, other financial assistance, medical and nursing home care, and support services to assist people in their homes. Benefits may be available for veterans with a **service-connected disability**, veterans whose income is low and who have a disability that is not service-connected, spouses, dependent children, and survivors. To be eligible for most benefits, you have to have seen active service and have a nondishonorable discharge. For information, see listing at end of this chapter.

TAX BREAKS FOR OLDER AMERICANS

Age plays a role in eligibility for some tax benefits. The following paragraphs highlight just a few of the special tax breaks for older persons or family members caring for aging parents. Talk to a tax adviser to explore how these may apply to your particular situation.

More generous filing requirements. The threshold for required filing of federal income tax returns is somewhat higher for older persons because of additional standard deductions for any person sixty-five or older or blind. For example, for tax year 1996, a single adult under sixty-five had to file a return if his or her gross income exceeded $6,550. But for a single person sixty-five or older, the threshold was $7,550. These exemptions and standard deductions are adjusted for inflation annually. Even if you are not *required* to file a tax return, do so if you have a refund coming for money withheld.

Claiming a parent as a dependent. An adult taxpayer may claim an older parent or other relative with little taxable income as a dependent, but the following requirements must be met:

- Over half the dependent's support for that calendar year must have been provided by the taxpayer.
- The dependent's gross income must be less than the exemption amount for the year in question (e.g., $2,500 in 1995).
- The dependent must not have filed a joint return with a spouse.
- The dependent must be an American citizen, resident, or national, or a resident of Canada or Mexico, for at least some part of the calendar year.

Usually, the claimed dependent is the taxpayer's parent, but other relatives can also be claimed, including aunts and uncles or even nonrelatives who meet the criteria.

Tax credit for dependent care. Employed taxpayers who care for an incapacitated parent, spouse, or other dependent in their homes may claim a tax credit for household or day care expenses that enable the taxpayer to be employed. The dependent's principal residence must be the taxpayer's household. Food and clothing costs are not allowable. However, the cost of care provided outside the home, such as in a day care center, is allowable even if food is included.

Tax credit for elderly and disabled. Persons sixty-five or older and persons with disabilities may be entitled to a tax credit if their nontaxable benefits or adjusted gross income falls below certain levels. You must file Form 1040 to claim the credit. You cannot claim it using form 1040EZ or Form 1040A.

Sale of personal residence. Formerly, federal law gave seniors a one-time exclusion of $125,000 on any gain realized in the sale of a personal residence. Tax law changes in 1997 now permit all homeowners to exclude up to $250,000 in gain from the sale of a principal residence ($500,000 for couples). The tax break is reusable every two years, although a host of rules complicates how this works.

Medical expenses. You may deduct the cost of medical care for yourself, spouse, and dependents if it exceeds 7.5 percent of your adjusted gross income. This deduction can be valuable for anyone with significant medical expenses in the family. Tax advisers and the IRS have detailed lists of eligible and ineligible expenses.

A note on tax planning. Tax planning is only one factor in planning for your later years. One transaction—such as the transfer of a home or property that has gained in value over the years—may have very different impacts under income tax rules and gift or estate tax rules. But apart from tax consequences, you will want to plan your affairs around your likely health and long-term care needs as well as your hopes and desires for living, loving, and growing even if the end of life is in sight. This is why a "holistic" approach to lifetime planning—one that takes into account more than just tax and legal technicalities—is especially appropriate for older adults.

WHERE TO GET MORE INFORMATION AND HELP

PENSIONS

- The U.S. Department of Labor, through its Pension and Welfare Benefits Administration, can provide information on private pensions and ERISA. Publications of interest include:

  How to Obtain Employee Benefit Documents from the Labor Department

  Can the Retiree Health Benefits Provided by Your Employer Be Cut?

Contact:

Pension and Welfare Benefits Administration (PWBA)
U.S. Department of Labor
Division of Technical Assistance and Inquiries
200 Constitution Avenue, NW
Washington, DC 20210
(202) 219-8776

The home page of the PWBA on the World Wide Web is http://dol.gov/dol/pwba. Their website includes information about their latest publications.

- For the publication *Things You Should Know About Your Pension Plan* and other information about the federal government insurance program protecting defined benefit pension plans, contact:

  Pension Benefit Guaranty Corporation
  P.O. Box 19153
  Washington, DC 20036
  (800) 400-PBGC

The home page of the PBGC on the World Wide Web is http://www.pbgc.gov.

- The **Internal Revenue Service** provides answers to many technical questions about pensions and retirement plans. If you have questions about specific provisions of tax laws affecting company and union pension plans, telephone the IRS Employee Plans Technical and Actuarial Division. IRS lawyers and actuaries respond to individual inquiries Monday through Thursday between 1:30 and 4:30 P.M., Eastern time. You can also write to the division for a free general-information letter. If you describe your situation, the IRS will explain the relevant sections of law. The IRS will not interpret the provisions of your pension plan.

  The home page of the IRS on the World Wide Web is http://www.irs.ustreas.gov. All IRS publications, forms, and newsworthy items may be found there, or you can call in your publication requests at their toll-free number: (800) 829-3676.

IRS publications of interest include:

Retirement Plans for Self-Employed Persons (Publication 560)

Tax Sheltered Annuity Programs for Employees of Public Schools and Certain Organizations (Publication 571)

Individual Retirement Arrangements (Publication 590)

Looking Out for #2: A Married Couple's Guide to Understanding Your Benefit Choices at Retirement from a Defined Contribution Plan (Publication 1565)

Looking Out for #2: A Married Couple's Guide to Understanding Your Benefit Choices at Retirement from a Defined Benefit Plan (Publication 1566)

- The **Pension Rights Center** has expertise on all aspects of pension law. The center's many publications include *The Pension Book* (available in bookstores), *Where to Look for Help with a Pension Problem,* and *Your Pension Rights at Divorce: What Women Need to Know.* Contact:

Pension Rights Center
918 Sixteenth Street, NW
Suite 704
Washington, DC 20006
(202) 296-3776.

Information about the Pension Rights Center may be found through the home page of the SPRY Foundation at http://www.spry.org.

- Other useful publications on pensions:

What You Should Know About Your Pension Rights and How to File a Claim for Your Benefits may be obtained (free) from the Consumer Information Center, Dept. 365-B, Pueblo, Co 81009. You can read the full *Consumer Information Catalog* on the World Wide Web at http://www.pueblo.gsa.gov.

Publications from the **American Association for Retired Persons** include *A Woman's Guide to Pension Rights* (D12258) and *Your Pension Plan: A Guide to Getting Through the Maze* (D13533). Order from AARP Fulfillment, 601 E Street, NW, Washington, DC 20049.

SOCIAL SECURITY, SSI, AND RAILROAD RETIREMENT

- (800) 772-1213 is the **Social Security Administration**'s nationwide toll-free number. It is available twenty-four hours a day with a Touch-Tone phone for automated services, or 7:00 A.M. to 7:00 P.M. to talk to a live representative. You can request an Earnings and Benefit Estimate Statement, general information pamphlets about Social Security, SSI, or railroad retirement, or other information over the phone. SSA also has free fact sheets explaining the government pension offset and windfall elimination rule.

- The IRS (see above) has free publications on the taxation of Social Security and railroad benefits, including *Older Americans'*

Tax Guide (Publication 544), and *Social Security and Equivalent Railroad Retirement Benefits* (Publication 915).

- *The Social Security Handbook* is a useful guide published annually by the Social Security Administration (SSA Publication No. 65-008). You may obtain it through Social Security offices, the U.S. Government Printing Office, or download it from the SSA's home page on the World Wide Web at http://www.ssa.gov.
- The **Railroad Retirement Board**'s home page on the World Wide Web is http://www.rrb.gov.

VETERANS' BENEFITS

- (800) 827-1000 is the toll-free information line of the U.S. **Department of Veterans Affairs**.
- The U.S. Department of Veterans Affairs publishes a yearly edition of *Federal Benefits for Veterans and Dependents*, available through VA offices, through the U.S. Government Printing Office in Washington, D.C., or through the Department of Veterans Affairs home page on the World Wide Web at http://www.va.gov.
- Also see *Veterans Benefits: The Complete Guide*, by Keith D. Snyder, Richard E. O'Dell, and Craig Kubey (New York: Harper Perennial, 1994).

CHAPTER THREE

Medicare and Private Health Benefits

THE FEDERAL GOVERNMENT PROVIDES a program of basic health care insurance for older and disabled persons called **Medicare.** Practically everyone sixty-five and older is eligible.

Don't confuse Medicare with **Medicaid,** which provides medical benefits for qualified *low-income* people. Medicare and Medicaid are not the same, though some older people qualify for both. Medicaid coverage rules vary from state to state, but Medicare is the same all over the United States.

This chapter examines Medicare, private "Medigap" insurance, and employer group coverage used to supplement Medicare coverage. Medicaid is covered in the next chapter.

Medicare has been revised many times. More revisions are likely. The most current information is usually available from your local Social Security Administration (SSA) office, and other organizations (see "Where to Get More Information and Help" at the end of the chapter).

MEDICARE

You are eligible for Medicare at age sixty-five even if you continue to work. Younger persons who have received Social Security disability benefits for more than twenty-four months are also eligible, as are persons who receive continuing dialysis for permanent kidney failure or who have had kidney transplants.

The **Health Care Financing Administration (HCFA)** is the federal agency responsible for administering Medicare. Medicare consists of two main parts. The "hospital insurance" part, or **Part A,** covers medically necessary care in hospitals and other facilities.

Part B, or the "medical insurance" part, covers medically necessary physician's services and a variety of other services and supplies not covered by Part A. Part B is also called **Supplementary Medical Insurance.** Home health care is covered by Part A or Part B, depending on the circumstances.

The specific coverage rules and limitations are complex. The actual coverage decisions and payments for care are handled by a variety of private insurance companies under contract with HCFA. When you receive hospital care, another group also plays an important role—**peer review organizations (PRO).** PROs are groups of doctors and other health care professionals paid by the federal government to monitor care given to Medicare patients, including the medical necessity for and the appropriateness and quality of hospital treatment.

Hospitals, doctors, and other health care providers can choose to participate in Medicare. Those that do are called **participating providers.** Most hospitals, nursing homes, and home health agencies participate, meet federal standards, and are certified as a Medicare-participating provider. Doctors have more flexibility, with the option of accepting or rejecting Medicare patients on a case-by-case basis. But even if doctors don't participate in Medicare, the government limits the fees they can charge Medicare patients.

Medicare beneficiaries also have the option of joining a **health maintenance organization (HMO)** or other **managed care plan** that participates in Medicare. Managed care organizations provide or arrange for all Medicare-covered services and generally charge a fixed monthly premium and small copayment (or no copayment) for services. They may offer benefits not covered by Medicare, such as prescription drug coverage or preventive care. However, managed care plans often restrict your choice of providers, your access to specialists, and your treatment options. Regular Medicare, in contrast, pays a **fee for service** to any qualified provider who renders medically necessary care.

WHAT DOES MEDICARE PART A COVER?

Medicare Part A helps pay for medically necessary hospital care, skilled nursing care, certain home health care, and hospice care.

Hospitalization. Under Medicare, a benefit period begins when you are hospitalized. In 1997, you have to pay an initial deductible of $760 (or less if the actual charges are less when you are admitted to a hospital). (Deductible amounts change each year.) Medicare then pays for all covered hospital care through day sixty. For the sixty-first through the ninetieth day, you have to pay $190 per day. After ninety days, you can choose to pay a coinsurance amount of $380 per day for up to sixty "lifetime reserve" days (or else pay the full charges yourself). Your **benefit period** ends sixty days after discharge from the hospital or skilled nursing bed. If another hospital admission occurs after that, you will have to pay another deductible, as well as the other cost-sharing amounts.

Hospitalization includes:

- a semiprivate room (two to four beds in a room);
- meals, including special diets;
- general nursing;
- special care units, such as an intensive care or a coronary care unit;

- drugs furnished by the hospital during your stay;
- blood transfusions;
- lab tests, X rays, and other radiology services such as radiation therapy;
- medical supplies and equipment, such as casts, dressings, and wheelchairs;
- operating room and recovery room costs;
- rehabilitation services, such as physical therapy, occupational therapy, and speech therapy;
- hospitalization in a participating psychiatric hospital, but this is limited to a lifetime maximum of 190 days. In most cases, psychiatric care in a general hospital is not subject to this limit.

These hospital services are *not covered:*

- Personal convenience items, such as telephone or televisions
- Private duty nurses
- Extra charges for a private room, unless a private room is medically necessary

Skilled nursing home care. Medicare covers *skilled* nursing facility inpatient care following a hospitalization of at least three days. Your condition must require, on a daily basis, skilled nursing or skilled rehabilitation services that, as a practical matter, can only be provided in a skilled nursing facility. You must be admitted within a short time (usually but not always thirty days) after you leave the hospital, and the skilled care you receive must be based on a doctor's order. If you qualify, you pay nothing for the first twenty days, except for any charges that Medicare does not allow. For the next eighty days, you pay charges up to $92 per day, and Medicare pays

SKILLED CARE OR CUSTODIAL CARE?

Medicare helps pay only for "skilled" nursing home care, not "custodial" care. However, the distinction is often fuzzy, and many Medicare denials based on a finding of custodial care can be successfully appealed. Generally, **custodial care** is primarily for helping the resident with daily living needs, such as eating, bathing, walking, getting in and out of bed, and taking medicine. **Skilled nursing** and **skilled rehabilitation services** require the skills of technical or professional personnel such as registered nurses, licensed practical nurses, or therapists. This may include observations, evaluation, and patient education.

all remaining allowable charges. No benefits are available after one hundred days of care in a "benefit period."

Most nursing home residents do not require the level of nursing services considered "skilled" by Medicare, so Medicare pays for relatively little nursing home care. In addition, not every nursing home participates in Medicare or is a skilled nursing facility. Ask the hospital discharge staff or nursing home staff if you are unsure of the facility's status.

If the requirements for skilled care coverage are met, Medicare covers:

- semiprivate room (two to four beds in a room);
- meals, including special diets;
- general nursing services;
- physical, occupational, and speech therapy;
- drugs furnished during your stay;
- medical supplies and equipment such as oxygen, casts, splints, and wheelchairs;

- routine personal hygiene items and services such as basic personal laundry, hair and nail hygiene care, combs, soap, specialized cleansing agents, lotions, toothbrush and toothpaste, denture supplies, deodorant, sanitary napkins, and incontinence care and supplies.

Home health care. Medicare covers part-time or intermittent skilled nursing; physical, occupational, and speech therapy services; medical social services; part-time care provided by a home health aide; and medical equipment for use in the home. It does not cover medications for patients living at home, nor does it cover general household services or services that are primarily custodial.

To be eligible, you must meet four conditions. First, you must be under the care of a physician who determines your need for home health care and sets up a plan. Second, you must be "homebound," although you need not be bedridden, and you may be able to leave your home with assistance. Third, the primary care you need must include part-time or intermittent skilled nursing, physical therapy, or speech therapy, although other services may be added to these. Fourth, your care must be provided by a Medicare-participating home health care agency. You are *not* required to have a hospital stay before home health services are covered. If you are in need of home health care, contact a home health agency. Hospital discharge planners will also make a referral.

Hospice care. A hospice provides pain relief, symptom management, and supportive services to people with terminal illness. Hospice services may include physician or visiting nurse services, individual and family psychological support, short-term inpatient care, home health aide services, drugs, and respite care. **Respite care** is short-term inpatient care (less than five consecutive days) in a facility to give family caregivers some relief. Respite care is available only on an occasional basis.

To be eligible for hospice care, the patient must be certified by a doctor as terminally ill (defined as a life expectancy of six months or less); the patient must choose to receive hospice care instead of standard Medicare benefits for the terminal illness; and the hospice must be a Medicare-participating program. Even while the patient receives hospice care, regular Medicare still helps pay for treatments not related to the terminal illness.

The hospice benefit is somewhat oddly structured around two ninety-day benefit periods, followed by a thirty-day period, and, if necessary, an extension period of indefinite duration (i.e., as long as the terminal condition lasts). You have the right to cancel hospice care at any time, but you lose any hospice days remaining during the benefit period you are in. For example, if you cancel at the end of sixty days in the first benefit period, the remaining thirty days are lost. However, you may still reelect hospice, because you have another ninety-day and a thirty-day benefit period (with indefinite extension) unused.

Medicare pays the hospice directly. You are responsible only for:

- 5 percent of the cost for outpatient prescription drugs, up to a maximum of $5 per prescription;
- $5 per day of inpatient respite care (this may change yearly and by geographic area).

WHAT DOES MEDICARE PART B COVER?

Medicare Part B covers a wide range of outpatient and physician expenses regardless of where they are provided—at home, in a hospital or nursing home, or in a private office. Covered services include:

- doctors' services, including some services by chiropractors, dentists, podiatrists, and optometrists;

- outpatient hospital services, such as emergency room services or outpatient clinic care, radiology services, and ambulatory surgical services;
- diagnostic tests, including X rays and other laboratory services, as well as some Pap smear screenings;
- durable medical equipment, such as oxygen equipment, wheelchairs, and other medically necessary equipment that your doctor prescribes for use in your home;
- kidney dialysis;
- ambulance services to or from a hospital or skilled nursing facility;
- certain services of other practitioners, such as clinical psychologists or social workers;
- under 1997 changes in the law, expanded preventive health care benefits for mammography, Pap smears, prostate and colorectal cancer screening, bone density measurement, and vaccines;
- many other health services, including home health care, medical supplies, and prosthetic devices not covered by Medicare Part A.

Part B does *not cover:*

- routine physical examinations;
- most routine foot care and dental care;
- examinations for prescribing or fitting eyeglasses or hearing aids;
- prescription drugs that do not require administration by a physician;
- most cosmetic surgery;
- immunizations except for certain persons at risk;

- personal comfort items and services;
- any service not considered "reasonable and necessary."

Call the insurance carrier that handles your medical claim to get answers to questions about specific cases.

WHAT IT COSTS YOU

Part A coverage is provided at no cost if you're sixty-five or older and eligible for Social Security. Part A is actually paid for out of payroll deductions from all wage earners' paychecks. If you are not eligible for Social Security benefits, you may still enroll in Part A after sixty-five, but you'll have to pay a sizable monthly premium. Part B is available to all Part A enrollees for a monthly premium that changes yearly. Under both Parts A and B, beneficiaries must pay certain deductibles and coinsurance payments, depending on the type of service. These amounts can change from year to year.

Your share of costs comes in three forms:

- **Premiums** (the regular monthly purchase price for Medicare Part B coverage)
- **Deductibles** (a payment made by you before Medicare begins paying for a service or supplies)

FOREIGN TRAVEL

Medicare generally does not pay for hospital or medical services outside the United States (Puerto Rico, the U.S. Virgin Islands, Guam, American Samoa, and the Northern Mariana Islands are considered part of the United States). There are certain emergency situations in Canada and Mexico in which Medicare will pay. When in doubt, ask your Medicare carrier.

- **Coinsurance** (sometimes called **copayments**—the part of a given expense for which you must pay, usually 20 percent of the Medicare-approved charge)

Private "Medigap" insurance covers all or part of these deductibles and copayments. Also, certain low-income beneficiaries may have them covered by Medicaid.

Under Part A, benefit limits and costs are based on a **benefit period.** At the beginning of each benefit period, a new cycle of benefits, deductibles, and coinsurance starts anew. A benefit period begins the first day you receive inpatient hospital

HELP FOR LOW-INCOME MEDICARE BENEFICIARIES.

If you are eligible for both Medicare and Medicaid, your state's Medicaid program will cover your share of Medicare costs and pay for many expenses not covered by Medicare. If your income is limited but you are *not* eligible for Medicaid, you may still qualify for help from Medicaid in paying your share of Medicare costs as a **Qualified Medicare Beneficiary (QMB)**. This will pay your Medicare Part B monthly premium and all Medicare deductibles and coinsurance. To be qualified for the QMB program, your financial assets (excluding your home, car, and certain other items) cannot exceed $4,000 for one person or $6,000 for a couple. And your income must be at or below the national poverty line, which is adjusted yearly. The 1997 poverty line for annual income is:

	Individual	*Couple*
Continental U.S.	$7,890	$10,610
Alaska	$9,870	$13,270
Hawaii	$9,070	$12,200

For individuals whose income is within 100 to 120 percent of the poverty line (or up to 150 percent if the state chooses), assistance is available under the **Specified Low-Income Medicare Beneficiary (SLMB)** program. This program pays only the monthly Medicare premium.

care. It ends when you have been out of a hospital and have not received skilled nursing care services for sixty days in a row. A subsequent hospitalization begins a new benefit period. Under Part B, benefits are more simply based on a calendar-year cycle. You are responsible for paying a $100 deductible for Part B benefits each calendar year before Medicare will pay any portion.

Your premiums, deductibles, and coinsurance amounts regularly change, some of them according to an annual inflation formula. Not surprisingly, costs always go up, never down.

MEDICARE BENEFIT AND COST SUMMARY—1997
PER BENEFIT PERIOD*

	Medicare Service	Medicare Pays	You or Your Medigap
PART A	**Hospital Inpatient**		
	Days 1–60	All costs after $760/stay deductible	$760/benefit period*
No monthly premium for most beneficiaries	Days 61–90	All costs after copayment	$190/day copayment
	Days 91–150 (once per lifetime)	All costs after copayment	$380/day copayment
	Days 151 and beyond	Nothing	All costs
	Skilled Nursing Home Care	(If patient meets "skilled" care conditions)	
	Days 1–20	All costs	Nothing
	Days 21–100	All costs after copayment	$95/day copayment
	Days 101 and higher	Nothing	All costs

	Medicare Service	Medicare Pays	You or Your Medigap
	Home Health Care **Skilled visits****	100% of approved amount if patient meets conditions	Nothing
	Hospice	All costs	Nothing
	210 days	Most costs for drugs and respite care	Small copayment
PART B			
Monthly premium: $43.80 (1997)	**Physician/Medical Expenses**	80% of approved amount after $100 deductible	20% of approved amount and charges above the approved amount
	Clinical Lab Services	100% of approved amount	Nothing
	Outpatient Hospital Treatment	80% of approved amount	20% of billed charges
	Most Outpatient Prescription Drugs	Nothing	All costs

*For **Part A,** a benefit period begins on the first day you receive services as an inpatient in a hospital and ends after you have been out of the hospital or a skilled nursing facility for sixty days in a row or remain in a skilled nursing care facility but do not receive care there for sixty days in a row. For **Part B,** a new benefit period begins each January 1.

**Home health care is also covered under Part B to the same extent.

Physician bills. If a physician charges you more than the Medicare-approved amount, the amount of your liability depends on whether he or she accepts **assignment.** Going to a doctor who accepts assignment will help you avoid excess charges. Accepting assignment means that the doctor agrees to accept the **Medicare-approved amount** as payment in full. The Medicare-approved amount is a fee schedule created by Medicare for every possible service or procedure. Your liability is limited to a coinsurance payment of 20 percent of the Medicare-approved amount. So if the Medicare-approved amount was $100 for a procedure, you would owe only $20 to a physician who accepts assignment.

A nonparticipating provider can charge you for the entire bill, including amounts over the Medicare-approved amount, but they cannot charge more than 15 percent over the Medicare-approved amount. Doctors cannot get around this limit. If they attempt to do so, they may be fined by the government.

At least eight states have laws that further limit what your doctor can charge you. These states include Connecticut, Massachusetts, Minnesota, New York, Ohio, Pennsylvania, Rhode Island, and Vermont. If you live in one of these states, call the Health Insurance Counseling Office for your state. You can find your state phone number through the national Medicare information line at (800) 638-6833.

If a doctor has charged you too much, ask for a reduction or a refund. The amount the doctor charges you should appear on the **Explanation of Medicare Part B Benefits** notice sent to you by Medicare. If there is any discrepancy, notify the Medicare carrier whose name appears on that form.

Physician bill example. Here is an example of the difference accepting assignment can make: Mrs. Jones sees Dr. Welby on June 1 for medical care. Dr. Welby normally charges $250 for such a visit. The Medicare-approved amount for such services is $200. Let's assume that Mrs. Jones has already met her $100 calendar-year deductible.

- *If Dr. Welby accepts assignment,* Mrs. Jones pays $40 copayment (in other words, 20 percent of the $200 approved amount). Dr. Welby submits the bill to Medicare and receives reimbursement for $160.
- *If Dr. Welby does* not *accept assignment,* he may require Mrs. Jones to pay the full bill up front, but the bill can be no higher than 15 percent over the Medicare-approved amount. Since the Medicare-approved amount is $200, the maximum he can charge is $230. Furthermore, *the doctor must submit the claim to the Medicare carrier on behalf of Mrs. Jones.* Mrs. Jones will receive a check from Medicare in the amount of $160 (80 percent of the $200 approved charge). Thus, Mrs. Jones's total out-of-pocket cost should be no more than $70 in this example (the $40 coinsurance plus the $30 maximum excess charge). Mrs. Jones will receive an **Explanation of Medicare Benefits** form explaining her obligation and rights.

OPTING FOR MEDICARE MANAGED CARE

Managed care plans have advantages and disadvantages. On the positive side, they provide all the covered Medicare benefits and usually more, and there is little or no paperwork to

FINDING A DOCTOR WHO ACCEPTS ASSIGNMENT

Doctors and suppliers who agree to accept assignment under Medicare on all claims are called **Medicare-participating** doctors and suppliers. Non-participating providers may still choose to accept assignment on a case-by-case basis. You can get a directory of them from your Medicare carrier. The directory is also available for your use in SSA offices, state and area agencies on aging, and in most hospitals.

deal with. Some plans charge a fixed monthly premium in addition to your Medicare Part B premiums or a small copayment each time you use a service, but many plans charge no additional costs. You do not pay any Medicare deductibles or coinsurance. The structure makes your health expenses more predictable and may eliminate the need for a "Medigap" policy. (But read the section on Medigap before considering dropping any Medigap policy you have.) Moreover, HMOs often provide benefits such as routine physicals, eye exams, inoculations, or prescription drugs, though exact additional services and costs vary substantially.

On the negative side, managed care plans generally require that you use their network of doctors and facilities. Usually, you will have a choice of primary care doctor, who oversees all your care, including serving as the gatekeeper for referrals to specialists and admission to a hospital (except in an emergency). Whether you can get services **"out-of-plan"**—that is, from a doctor or other provider not a member of the plan—depends on the type of plan you are in. HMOs usually have one of three policies:

- Some plans have **"lock-in" requirements** that restrict you to receiving *all* covered care through the plan or through referral by the plan. If you receive services out-of-plan, neither the managed care organization nor Medicare will cover the service, unless it is an emergency or urgently needed care.
- Some plans offer a **"point-of-service" option,** under which you receive certain services outside the provider's network. However, you will pay more of the cost than you would if you had gone to a provider within your HMO.
- Some plans give you the choice of receiving care in-plan or going out-of-plan to any provider under the regular Medicare fee-for-service rules. If you go out-of-plan, you are responsible for all the Medicare deductibles, coinsurance, and other charges.

Your **state insurance counseling office** can tell you about available plans in your area. It can be quite confusing to compare plan benefits, costs, services, and quality, so seek help in evaluating your options. All plans available under Medicare have open enrollment periods of at least thirty days once per year. Plans cannot reject Medicare beneficiaries because of poor health.

Once you join a managed care plan, you can stay in it as long as it remains approved by Medicare, or you can leave at any time to join another plan or return to the regular Medicare fee-for-service program. To change from one HMO to another, you simply enroll in the new HMO. To disenroll and return to the regular fee-for-service arrangement, send a signed request to the plan or to your local Social Security office. You will revert back to fee-for-service Medicare on the first day of the month after your request was received.

EMERGENCY CARE OUTSIDE YOUR HMO

Your HMO must pay for emergency care and for unforeseen, urgently needed, out-of-area care you get from non-HMO health care providers, including necessary follow-up care.

- **Emergencies** are situations in which you need medical care immediately because of sudden or suddenly worsening illness or injury, and it seems to you that if you take the time to reach your plan doctor or hospital, you risk permanent damage to your health.
- **Urgent care** situations are when you have an unexpected illness or injury while you are temporarily outside the HMO's service area. Your HMO must cover the care if you are temporarily away from the HMO service area and your illness or injury is unexpected and requires medical care that cannot be delayed until you return home.

In either case, if coverage is declined, consider appealing that decision.

If you drop out of a Medicare HMO to go back to regular Medicare, be sure you have, or can get, an adequate "Medigap" policy. If you have any preexisting medical conditions, many insurance companies will not sell you a Medigap policy or will impose a waiting period for those conditions.

SIGNING UP FOR MEDICARE

Enrolling in Medicare is easy. Everyone who is turning sixty-five and applying for Social Security or railroad retirement benefits is automatically enrolled in Medicare Parts A and B. If you don't want Part B coverage (perhaps because you have good company retiree health benefits), you must notify the SSA. If you are one of the few not eligible for Medicare, you can purchase the coverage, but the premium for Part A is fairly costly. If you are receiving Social Security retirement or railroad retirement benefits before age sixty-five, you should automatically receive a Medicare card prior to the month you turn sixty-five. The Medicare benefits normally begin on the first of the month in which you turn sixty-five. If you are under sixty-five and receiving Social Security disability benefits, your enrollment in Medicare will begin automatically as soon as you have been receiving disability benefits for twenty-four months. Once your benefits start, your Part B premium will be deducted from your monthly Social Security check.

If you have not applied for Social Security or railroad retirement because you are planning to work beyond age sixty-five or for any other reason, you must file a written Medicare application through your local SSA office when you decide to enroll. You must apply during an enrollment period. Your "initial" enrollment period begins three calendar months before your sixty-fifth birthday month, and extends three months beyond your birthday month. You can enroll at any time during this seven-month period. If you delay enrollment beyond this initial period because you are in a group health plan, you will have a special enrollment period, beginning on the first day of the month in which you are no longer in a group health plan. The special period lasts seven months after you are no longer enrolled. If you do not enroll during either of these periods, you can enroll during "general" enrollment periods, which run from January 1 to March 31 of each year. However, you will pay a higher monthly premium if you delay enrollment beyond your initial enrollment period. Each year you delay results in a further increase in premium.

Many persons on Medicare continue to be covered by an employer's health insurance program, either because they or their spouses are still employed or otherwise eligible for employer coverage. In these cases, Medicare is the **secondary payer** of covered medical expenses *after* the other insurance pays out its benefits. To make sure you receive maximum coverage, talk to your employer's benefits office or your local SSA office.

THE CLAIMS PROCESS: HOW ARE MEDICARE CLAIMS FILED AND PAID?

For Part A benefits, providers submit claims directly to Medicare's **fiscal intermediary** (a private insurance company under contract for your geographic area). The provider will charge you for any deductible or coinsurance payment you owe.

For Part B claims, doctors, suppliers, and other providers are required to submit your Medicare claims to the **Medicare carrier** (an insurance company that may be the same as or different from the fiscal intermediary for Part A). Your doctor cannot legally ask you to sign any agreement waiving this filing obligation. A participating provider can charge you directly for any deductible or coinsurance. A nonparticipating provider can charge you for the entire bill, including amounts over the Medicare-approved amount, as long as the excess charge does not exceed the limit set by Medicare, as explained earlier.

After your doctor or other Part B provider or supplier sends in a claim to Medicare, you will receive in the mail a notice called an **Explanation of Medicare Part B Benefits** to tell you what Medicare is covering on the claim. This is an important notice, because it tells you:

- the name of the provider, type of service, date, and cost;
- the amount Medicare is paying;
- the amount you are responsible for, including information about your annual deductible;
- whether your physician or other provider has accepted assignment;
- information about appealing any aspect of the Medicare determination with which you disagree (explained on back of the form).

If you belong to a Medicare-participating health maintenance organization (HMO), there are usually no claim forms to be filed, and often no deductible or copayment for any covered services.

POTENTIAL TROUBLE AREAS UNDER MEDICARE

These are potential problem situations under Medicare you should always consider challenging.

Early discharge from the hospital. You should never be told that you are being discharged because your hospital coverage under Medicare is running out. If you have a medical need for hospitalization, your coverage should continue, although your copayment responsibilities kick in after sixty days. Misunderstandings often arise because of the way hospitals are paid.

Medicare pays for most inpatient hospital care under the **Prospective Payment System (PPS)**. Under this system, hospitals receive a fixed payment based on your primary diagnosis at admission. The diagnosis categories are called **Diagnosis Related Groups,** or **DRGs,** and they are based upon an average cost for treating your type of diagnosis. If your stay is shorter than the norm, the hospital makes money from the DRG payment. If your stay is longer than the norm or your treatment was especially complicated, the hospital may lose money on your particular stay. The incentive under this system is obvious. But, in all cases, the decision to discharge should be based only on medical necessity and not on the payment rules.

Discharge before a skilled nursing bed in the area is found. Medicare law provides for continued hospital care when no appropriate skilled nursing facility bed is available in the area. The main burden of locating a skilled nursing facility is on the treating physician and hospital discharge planner. The nursing home must be reasonably close to home and family.

Denial of skilled nursing facility coverage. Most denials are based on a determination by the nursing home that skilled care is not medically necessary. Sometimes, nursing homes interpret too narrowly the services that are considered skilled. They may ignore Medicare rules that require the review of your overall condition.

Home health care early terminations. Often, patients are told that there is a time limit on home health coverage. Medicare has no absolute time limit on home health care coverage. Instead, Medicare requires that the person need skilled nursing or rehabilitation on a part-time (generally up to eight hours per day) or intermittent basis (generally, less than seven days per week, or even if seven days a week, for a time-limited period). The "homebound" requirement for home health coverage also creates disputes. You can leave home, with assistance, for medical appointments, adult day care, for other occasional purposes, and still be considered homebound.

"No improvement" denials. Physical, occupational, and speech therapy are sometimes improperly terminated when further medical improvement is no longer possible. If skilled therapy is needed to prevent or delay further deterioration or to preserve current capabilities, the service should be covered.

IF YOU DISAGREE WITH MEDICARE . . . APPEAL!

Remember, you have the right to appeal all decisions regarding coverage or services or the amount Medicare will pay on a claim. Consider appealing even partial denials, especially if the basis of denial is unclear. A substantial percentage of claims are successful on appeal. Even if unsuccessful, the appeal may make clear the reason for the denial.

The starting point is getting an initial determination. *Do not accept an oral notice of denial or termination of services.* You are not obligated for a bill until you receive proper written notice. If the notice is merely the provider's opinion, then it is not an official determination. You should ask the provider to get an official Medicare determination. The provider must file a claim on your behalf to Medicare if you ask for an official determination. Then, if you still disagree,

OFFERS OF "FREE" SERVICES OR EQUIPMENT OR DEALS YOU CAN'T REFUSE

Be suspicious of anyone offering free screenings, testing, or medical equipment in exchange for your Medicare number, or being told that you will not have to pay the normal 20 percent coinsurance. These may be signs of fraudulent operations. If you suspect fraud, call your Medicare carrier or intermediary (whose name and number will be on any Explanation of Medicare Benefits form) or the Medicare hotline at (800) 638-6833.

you may make use of several appeal steps if the required minimum amounts of money are in dispute. (The process is somewhat different if you are enrolled in a Medicare-managed care organization.)

Unfortunately, the appeals process may take many months if you have to go beyond the first stage of appeal. At any stage that you receive an unfavorable decision, you have a time limit for appealing to the next stage. You may lose your rights if you wait too long. For most steps in the appeals process, you have sixty days from the date of receiving the notice to submit your appeal request. Always put your appeal request in writing. To ask for Part B reviews and hearings by the carrier (i.e., insurance company, not the Social Security Administration), you have six months. Hospital decisions should be appealed immediately, since time is of the essence.

APPEALS OF HOSPITAL DENIALS

Starting point. Hospital coverage decisions are normally made by **Peer Review Organizations (PROs),** groups of doctors and other health care professionals that review care given to Medicare patients. When you are admitted to the hospital, you should receive a notice titled **An Important Message from Medicare: Your Rights While You Are a Medicare Hospital Patient**

> **DENIALS OF BENEFITS**
>
> Medicare Consumer Commandment Number 1 is to *never accept a denial of benefits without further questioning.* Unfair denials of Medicare benefits occur with surprising frequency. Medicare beneficiaries who appeal unfair denials have a substantial likelihood of success on appeal.

that explains the role of PROs (Peer Review Organizations) and describes your appeal rights. When hospital coverage is being terminated, you must receive a written **Notice of Noncoverage** that again explains how to appeal.

Appeals Steps

1. Immediately request a **review** of the decision by the PRO. If you request a review by noon of the first working day after you received the hospital denial notice, then you will normally receive a decision by the close of business on the following day. If you appeal in this time limit, the hospital cannot charge you for inpatient services provided before noon of the day following the day you receive the PRO decision.
2. Request a **reconsideration** by the PRO.
3. Request a **hearing** (if at least $200 in benefits is in dispute). Hearings are conducted by independent administrative law judges (ALJs) through the SSA.
4. Request a **review by the Appeals Council** of the SSA (if at least $2,000 in benefits is in dispute).
5. File for **judicial review** in U.S. District Court (if at least $2,000 in benefits is in dispute).

APPEALS OF NURSING HOME, HOME HEALTH AGENCY, AND HOSPICE DECISIONS

Starting point. The provider must give you a written **Notice of Noncoverage** explaining why the provider believes Medicare will not cover the service. This is not an official Medicare determination. You have the right to ask the provider to file the claim and get an official Medicare determination. Once this is done, you will get a **Notice of Utilization** from Medicare giving you an official decision and explaining your right to appeal.

Appeals Steps

1. Request a **reconsideration** by the intermediary (the insurance company handling the claim for Medicare).
2. Request a **hearing** (if at least $100 in benefits is in dispute). Hearings are conducted by independent administrative law judges (ALJs) through the SSA.
3. Request a **review by the Appeals Council** of the SSA (if at least $1,000 in benefits is in dispute).
4. File for **judicial review** in U.S. District Court (if at least $1,000 in benefits is in dispute).

APPEALS OF DECISIONS REGARDING PHYSICIAN SERVICES OR OTHER PART B SERVICES AND SUPPLIERS

Starting point. Part B providers must file claim forms for you. You will receive an **Explanation of Medicare Benefits** form in the mail from the carrier (the insurance company handling the claim for Medicare). The form will explain what Medicare is covering, the amount, and your appeal rights.

Appeals Steps

1. Request a **review by the carrier.**
2. Request a **hearing before a carrier hearing officer** (if at least $100 in benefits is in dispute. You may combine several claims).
3. Request a **hearing** (if at least $500 in benefits is in dispute) by an independent administrative law judge (ALJ) through the SSA.
4. Request a **review of the Appeals Council** of the SSA (if at least $1,000 in benefits is in dispute).
5. File for **judicial review** in U.S. District Court (if at least $1,000 in benefits is in dispute).

APPEALS OF DECISIONS MADE BY MANAGED CARE ORGANIZATIONS

Starting point. If you have Medicare coverage through a health maintenance organization (HMO) or other managed care organization, your HMO will usually make all decisions about services and coverage. If the decision is one which jeopardizes your health or ability to regain maximum function, the appeals process must be expedited, generally within 72 hours.

Appeals Steps

1. Request a **reconsideration** by the HMO. If the HMO does not fully rule in your favor, it must send your reconsideration request to the Health Care Financing Administration's review contractor for examination. The contractor, known as the **Center for Health Dispute Resolution,** reviews the case and provides you written notice of its decision.
2. Request a **hearing** (if at least $100 in benefits is in dispute) before an independent administrative law judge (ALJ) through the SSA.
3. Request a **review by the Appeals Council** of the SSA (if at least $1,000 in benefits is in dispute).
4. File for **judicial review** in U.S. District Court (if at least $1,000 in benefits is in dispute).

Pursuing an appeal takes some patience and persistence, but it often pays off. Many people handle Medicare appeals on their own. Getting the provider to submit additional information often results in approval of the claim. However, each step in the appeals process gets more complicated. You will be in a stronger position if you have the support of your doctor and representation by or help from an attorney or a trained paralegal, benefits specialist, or trained outreach worker. See chapter 11 for suggestions on finding legal assistance.

Your employee benefits package may include a promise to provide benefits to you after you retire. These benefits are particularly important to you if you retire before sixty-five, because until sixty-five, you are not eligible for Medicare. Even if you are over sixty-five, employer coverage might save you a lot on Medigap policies.

The shrinking of retiree benefits. Unfortunately, many employers have reduced or even eliminated benefits after employees have retired. Or they have increased the retirees' share of the cost. Employers have the right to make these cutbacks if the health plan gives them authority to change or discontinue benefits. Health benefits do not **vest** as pension benefits do, and unless the employer made an unqualified contract with employees, you could lose your benefits.

Health benefits when you lose your job. If you are laid off, terminated, or are leaving your job, but not retiring, you and your dependents may be eligible to continue your group plan benefits under a federal law known as COBRA. These benefits are available for a limited period of time (usually eighteen months, but up to twenty-nine months for a person determined disabled under the Social Security Act), and premiums must be paid by you, not the employer. You get coverage under COBRA at the group plan rates, usually much lower than the cost of individual health insurance. COBRA provisions are complex. Be sure to get information from your employer or your health plan or an attorney knowledgeable about COBRA.

If you leave your job and then obtain a new one, you may benefit from a new federal law designed to make benefits more portable. The law says that "preexisting condition" waiting periods can be no more than twelve months. (A **preexisting condition** is any condition for which medical advice was sought or treatment was recommended during the six months before your enrollment date). Moreover, this exclusion period must be reduced by any period of time you had coverage under another health plan as long as there has been no gap in employer or COBRA coverage of sixty-three days or longer. Thus, for many job changes, your prior coverage may totally eliminate any waiting periods.

"MEDIGAP" INSURANCE

Medicare provides basic health care coverage but leaves many gaps. Most older persons need to purchase a supplemental (or "Medigap") insurance policy to cover some of the costs not insured by Medicare. These policies do *not* cover long-term care. Long-term-care insurance is discussed in the next chapter.

While most people need Medigap coverage, you may already have enough coverage without it if you belong to one of the four groups below:

1. If you are already covered by **Medicaid,** you do not need a Medigap policy. Medicaid covers the gaps in Medicare and more.

THE CHANGING FACE OF MEDICARE

Changes made by Congress to Medicare in 1997 will create some new coverage choices for seniors in the near future, such as the use of "Medical Savings Accounts" and new managed care options such as **Provider Sponsored Organizations (PSOs)** and **Preferred Provider Organizations (PPOs)**. As with any new health product, approach these cautiously and get full information about them if they become available in your area. Call the Health Insurance Counseling Program in your state for help. See "Where to Get More Information and Help" at the end of this chapter.

2. If you are not eligible for Medicaid, but your income is low, you may be eligible for help in paying Medicare costs under the **Qualified Medicare Beneficiary (QMB)** program. Under QMB, the government will pay your Medicare Part B premiums and provide supplemental coverage equivalent to a Medigap policy if your income and assets fall below a qualification amount (one that is more generous than Medicaid's). See page 55 for more details about QMB. To apply, contact the local office of your state Medicaid program.
3. If you get **retiree health coverage** through a former employer or union, you *may* not need Medigap insurance. But this coverage may not provide the same benefits as Medigap insurance and may not have to meet the federal and state rules that apply to Medigap. Examine the coverage, costs, and stability of your coverage to determine whether it is a better option than Medigap.
4. If you belong to an **HMO,** you probably do not need a Medigap policy, since HMO coverage is normally comprehensive. But do not be too quick to give up your Medigap coverage if you are just joining a Medicare HMO. If you can afford it, keep it long enough to be sure you are satisfied with the HMO. If you become dissatisfied with the HMO, you have the right to disenroll from it at any time. But if you have already given up your Medigap coverage, you may not be able to get it again or get the same price.

SHOP FOR A GOOD MEDIGAP POLICY

Since 1992, all Medigap insurance has had to conform to standardized benefit plans. There are ten possible standardized plans, identified as Plan A through Plan J. Plan A is a core package and is available in all states. The other nine plans have different combinations of benefits. Check with your state department of insurance for additional information. Many states provide buyers' guides.

Purchase only one Medigap policy. Multiple policies will almost always provide overlapping coverage for which you will pay twice but receive the benefit only once. In evaluating policies, decide which features would best meet your health needs and financial situation. Prescription drug coverage, for example, may be right for you if you are on continuing maintenance medications, even though such coverage may be expensive. When you compare policies of the same type (A through J), remember that benefits are identical for plans of the same type. For example, all Type G plans have essentially the same benefits. However, the premiums and potential for premium increases may differ greatly.

Companies commonly use one of three methods for setting Medigap premiums. Many set the premiums at the **issue age**—your age on the date you buy the policy. For example, if you buy the policy at sixty-five, you will always pay the premium that a sixty-five-year-old pays. However, if the rate for all sixty-five-year-olds goes up, your premium rate will go up, too. Other companies set premiums according to your **attained age,** meaning your current age. These premiums increase automatically each year. These policies may appear cheaper initially, but they could cost much more later on. Finally, a few companies charge one **standard premium** for all policyholders, regardless of age. These policies might be a better deal if you apply for Medigap at an older age. The best way to compare premium costs is to project the likely cost of the policy over several years.

When to get Medigap. Buy a Medigap policy at or near the time your Medicare coverage begins, because during the first six months that you are sixty-five or older *and* enrolled in Medicare Part B, companies must accept you regardless of any health conditions you have, and they cannot charge you more than they charge others of the same age. After this one-time period, you may be forced to pay much higher premiums for the same policy due to your health status. During this open enrollment period, companies may still exclude **pre-existing conditions** during the first six months of the policy.

Different enrollment rules apply to persons under sixty-five who are eligible for Medicare because of disability.

What if I have an "old" Medigap policy? If you have a Medigap policy that predates the standardized plans (before 1992), you may not need to switch policies, especially if you are satisfied. Some states have special regulations allowing beneficiaries to convert older policies to a standard Medigap plan. Check with your state insurance department or health insurance counseling service for details.

Beware of illegal sales practices. Both federal and state laws govern the sale of Medigap insurance. These laws prohibit high-pressure sales tactics, fraudulent or misleading statements about coverage or cost, selling a policy that is not one of the approved standard policies, or imposing new waiting periods for replacement policies. If a sales agent offers you a policy that duplicates coverage of your existing policy, the duplication must be disclosed to you in writing. If you feel you have been misled or pressured, contact your state insurance department, your state's health insurance counseling program, or the federal Medicare information line at (800) 638-6833.

WHERE TO GET MORE INFORMATION AND HELP

MEDICARE AND MEDIGAP

- Any Social Security Administration office can answer most questions about Medicare enrollment, coverage, and premiums, or help you replace a lost Medicare card. Social Security offices also carry informational publications produced by the **Health Care Financing Administration (HCFA).** You also can obtain a tremendous amount of information on the Internet from HCFA—their World Wide Web address is http://www.hcfa.gov.

Some of the materials available from the Health Care Financing Administration:

- *Your Medicare Handbook* (Pub. No. HCFA 10050), revised annually, is available on HCFA's website or can be purchased.
- *Guide to Health Insurance for People with Medicare* is a free booklet available from your local Social Security Administration or from the Consumer Information Center, Department 70, Pueblo, CO 81009, (719) 948-3334 (Internet site is http://www.pueblo.gsa.gov). It is also available on the HCFA website (page 75). It explains how Medigap insurance works, explains the ten standardized plans, tells how to shop for Medigap insurance, and lists addresses and phone numbers of state insurance departments and state agencies on aging. Most states offer free insurance counseling services.
- *What Medicare Beneficiaries Need to Know About Health Maintenance Organizations (HMO) Arrangements: Know Your Rights* provides an excellent overview of managed care options and consumer rights.

- **Health Insurance Counseling Programs.** Every state, plus Puerto Rico, the Virgin Islands, and the District of Columbia, has a health insurance counseling program that can give you free information and help on Medicare, Medicaid, Medigap, and other health insurance benefits. To find the program in your state, call your local area agency on aging, your state insurance division, or your Social Security office. The *Guide to Health Insurance for People with Medicare* (described above) also lists these programs.

- *Medicare & Medigap Update* (revised annually). Published by the United Seniors Health Cooperative, 1331 H Street, NW, Suite 500, Washington, DC 20005-4706. This booklet provides consumer advice on Medicare and Medigap insurance. Call (202) 393-6222 for ordering information, or visit their website at http://www.ushc-online.org.

CHAPTER FOUR

Medicaid and Long-Term-Care Benefits

MEDICAID IS A MEDICAL ASSISTANCE PROGRAM for low-income older or disabled persons. The program also covers certain younger persons receiving welfare payments under what used to be called Aid to Families with Dependent Children (AFDC) but is now known as Temporary Assistance to Needy Families (TANF). Unlike Medicare, which offers the same benefits to all enrollees regardless of income, Medicaid is managed by individual states, and the benefits and eligibility rules vary from state to state.

Medicaid also benefits many middle-income individuals faced with the devastating costs of nursing home care. However, the rules for eligibility and coverage are complex and are variable from state to state, and the operation of the program is often bureaucratic and frustrating.

This chapter provides a general overview of Medicaid, including its special rules of coverage for nursing home care. We then explain the option of purchasing private insurance to pay for long-term care.

WHAT MEDICAID COVERS

Certain Medicaid benefits are mandated by federal law. They include:

- inpatient and outpatient hospital services;
- doctors' and nurse practitioners' services;
- nursing home care;
- rural health clinic services;
- home health care services;
- laboratory and X-ray charges;
- transportation to and from health care providers.

Other services states *may* cover include: private duty nursing; services from podiatrists, optometrists, and chiropractors; mental health services; personal care in your home; dental care; physical therapy and other rehabilitation; prescription medications; dentures; eyeglasses; and more. In all cases, you may receive these services only from a Medicaid-participating provider. As with Medicare, providers may choose whether or not to participate in Medicaid, and they must meet certain standards.

WHO'S ELIGIBLE FOR MEDICAID?

Medicaid programs in each state have different eligibility standards. All states require that adults without dependent children be at least sixty-five, blind, or disabled, *and* that they meet income and asset tests.

The **income tests** are linked to the federal Supplemental Security Income (SSI) program or, for younger applicants, to Temporary Assistance to Needy Families (TANF). In most states, persons eligible for SSI or TANF are automatically covered. These are **categorically eligible** individuals. Most states also cover some people whose income falls below a certain level after they "spend down" a portion of their income on medical bills. These are called **medically needy** individuals. Finally, some states set a gross-income eligibility gap for certain benefits—specifically, nursing home care—at three times the maximum SSI benefit for a single individual. This cap changes yearly, since the SSI maximum benefit is adjusted yearly for inflation. (For example, the SSI maximum payment for 1997 was $484. Thus, in 1997, the income cap was $1,452 in these states.) An individual who is even $1 over the income cap is ineligible, no matter how high his or her medical bills are. As of this writing, the states that impose an **income cap** on eligibility for nursing home care are:

Alabama	Florida	Oklahoma
Alaska	Idaho	Oregon
Arizona	Iowa	South Carolina
Arkansas	Louisiana	South Dakota
Colorado	Mississippi	Texas
Delaware	Nevada	Wyoming
	New Mexico	

Medicaid also imposes an **asset** or **resource test**. In most states, the resource eligibility limits are $2,000 for an individual and $3,000 for married couples, although these amounts may vary. As with SSI, not all resources are counted under the resource test. The resources *not* counted include:

- your home, as long as you live in it, or expect to return to it, or your spouse lives in it;
- most household goods and personal effects (at least up to $2,000 worth) and wedding rings;
- an automobile (up to $4,500 in fair market value, or no limit if needed for employment);
- cash value of life insurance, *if* the face value is less than $1,500 (if the face value is higher, the cash value is counted as an asset);

- trade/business property needed for self-support (e.g., tools, machinery);
- value of burial plot;
- up to $1,500 in a burial expense fund (this is simply any account earmarked for burial expenses).

Special income and asset rules apply to persons who need help paying nursing home bills. These rules are so complicated that you should talk with someone with expertise in Medicaid—such as a legal services lawyer, benefits counselor at a senior center or health insurance counseling office, paralegal, social worker, or private attorney experienced in handling Medicaid issues.

You may receive both Medicare and Medicaid. Even if you do not qualify for Medicaid, the Medicaid program may still help you pay for all or part of your Medicare expenses if you meet the special income and resource tests under the **Qualified Medicare Beneficiary (QMB)** program or the **Specified Low-Income Medicare Beneficiary (SLMB)** (see page 55).

IMMIGRANT RESTRICTIONS

Federal laws passed in 1996 barred almost all current and future immigrants who had not become citizens from receiving most federal and some state funded services and benefits designed to assist low-income persons (including Supplemental Security Income, Medicaid, and food stamps). In 1997, Congress reinstated eligibility for SSI and Medicaid for most legal immigrants residing in the United States as of August 22, 1996. Legal immigrants arriving after August 22, 1996, are barred from receiving benefits unless they meet very strict guidelines. The immigrant restrictions are complex, vary according to a person's immigration category and the benefits or services in question, and are subject to change.

MEDICAID—GOOD NEWS AND BAD NEWS

No other program pays for as broad a range of benefits as Medicaid. And once you are eligible, Medicaid requires no premiums or deductibles like Medicare (although a nominal copayment can be required for some benefits such as prescription drugs). Doctors or other providers can't charge you additional fees beyond the Medicaid reimbursement amount. The nursing home benefit is especially valuable, because Medicaid is the only program that covers significant amounts of nursing home care. Private long-term-care insurance is emerging as an important resource, but it is still a small player in the system.

But there are disadvantages. You must be virtually impoverished before you qualify for Medicaid. Those who become eligible after "spending down" their income or assets discover that little is left over. Once you're eligible, finding a doctor who participates in Medicaid may not be easy. Finding a nursing home bed for a Medicaid patient is tougher, too. Medicaid beneficiaries have fewer choices and less flexibility in meeting their health care needs than do persons with private insurance. Finally, since late 1993, Congress has required states to seek reimbursement of Medicaid payments for nursing home and other long-term-care costs from estates of deceased Medicaid beneficiaries.

APPLYING FOR MEDICAID

Before applying, consult with someone with expertise in Medicaid. Then, contact the state or local agency that handles Medicaid. Its name will vary from place to place. It may be called the Department of Social Services, Public Aid, Public Welfare, Human Services, or something similar. You can also call your local agency on aging or senior center for information.

When you apply, you will need to document your financial circumstances in detail, as well as your residency. The application form can be complex, but the Medicaid agency can help you complete it. If you are homebound, a Medicaid worker can come to your home to help you apply. If you are in a hospital or other institution, a staff social worker can help you apply. Since the start of benefits is linked to your date of application, establish an application date as soon as you need Medicaid assistance. (In certain instances, coverage may be retroactive up to three months before your date of application.) Almost any written request with your signature is enough to establish your application date, even if you have not yet completed the full application form.

If you disagree with Medicaid . . . appeal! You have the right to appeal all decisions that affect your Medicaid eligibility or services. You should receive prompt written notice of any decision about your Medicaid coverage. This will include an explanation of how you can appeal. The appeal process differs slightly from state to state, but it always includes a right to a fair hearing before a hearing officer. You don't need legal representation, but it's a good idea to get help from a public benefits specialist or a lawyer experienced in Medicaid law.

MEDICAID COVERAGE OF LONG-TERM CARE

Medicaid pays about half of the nation's nursing home bill, but only for the virtually broke. Because nursing homes cost about $35,000 per year (and double that in some urban areas), it is easy to become penniless fast. Medicaid will cover nursing home expenses if your condition requires nursing home care, the home is certified by the state Medicaid agency, and you meet income and other eligibility requirements.

Other federal programs pay very little for nursing home care. For example, Medicare coverage is narrowly defined and limited to twenty days of full coverage and a maximum of eighty additional days with a large coinsurance payment. The Department of Veterans Affairs (DVA) pays for some nursing home care for veterans, but the benefit is limited to available resources and facilities. Priority is given to veterans with medical problems related to their military service (**service-connected disabilities**), to very old veterans of wartime service, and to very poor veterans. Contact your local VA office for more information.

A Medicaid nursing home impoverishment example: Mrs. Smith enters a nursing home, having an income of $1,200 per month and $50,000 in savings. The nursing home private pay rate is $3,000 per month, and Mrs. Smith's additional incidental expenses amount to $100 per month. She will spend down her savings at a rate of $1,900 per month (i.e., $1,200 in income + $1,900 in savings are needed to meet the monthly total expense of $3,100). At this rate, Mrs. Smith's savings are depleted down to the Medicaid asset level ($2,000) in just over two years. Many persons who are not eligible for Medicaid become eligible, like Mrs. Smith, after a period of time in a nursing home. The rules in this situation vary considerably from state to state.

The rest of this chapter looks at options that may delay the need for a nursing home and lessen the impoverishment caused by long-term-care costs and Medicaid eligibility.

HOW MEDICAID PAYS

Medicaid providers bill Medicaid directly. The state Medicaid program reimburses providers. Providers cannot charge you additional amounts for covered services unless the state program requires a nominal copayment for the services. Medicaid will not reimburse you for the charges you paid.

HOME- AND COMMUNITY-BASED SERVICES

Medicaid in your state may cover a variety of home- and community-based services, including home health, homemaker, home health aide, and personal care services (help with normal activities of daily living, such as dressing, bathing, toileting, eating, and walking).

Many states also have instituted Medicaid "waiver" programs that allow the state to use Medicaid dollars for home- and community-based services that normally would not be covered under Medicaid. These programs usually target persons who might otherwise have to live in a nursing home. Services may include personal care, adult day care, housekeeping services, care management, chore and companion services, and respite care that enables caregivers to take a break from their responsibilities. Check with your local office on aging or department of human services about the options available in your state.

LIFETIME CHANCES OF BEING IN A NURSING HOME
(If you are now 65 years old)

Length of Stay	Men	Women
Never Enter	67%	48%
Less than 12 months	19%	21%
1 to 5 years	10%	18%
More than 5 years	4%	13%

Source: *New England Journal of Medicine, February 1991,* "Lifetime Use of Nursing Home Care," by P. Kemper and C. Murtaugh.

If your spouse resides in or will be entering a nursing home, Medicaid has special rules that allow the **community spouse** (spouse remaining in the community) to keep more income and assets than permitted under the regular eligibility rules. The specifics vary from state to state, but here is the general structure.

Income rules. The community spouse can keep all income, no matter how much, that belongs exclusively to the community spouse. Joint income is treated differently. The state will require part, and possibly all, of it to help pay nursing home expenses.

Most of the income of the nursing home spouse is considered available to pay for nursing home care. However, part of the nursing home spouse's income may be used by the community spouse as a **minimum monthly maintenance needs allowance** if the community spouse's income is below an amount set by the state. Just enough monthly income—or sometimes assets—are taken from the nursing home spouse to bring the income of the community spouse up to an income level set by the state. The amount must be at least 150 percent of the poverty level for a two-person household, but no higher than a cap set by federal law. (In 1997, the *minimum* spousal allowance was $1,326 per month, with the *maximum* set at $1,976. The amounts are higher in Alaska and Hawaii.) States can set the level anywhere within this range. If the state's allowance is less than the maximum, it may be increased to cover **shelter costs** (rent, mortgage, taxes, insurance, and utilities) that exceed a specified amount. Additional allowances are made for dependent children.

Resource rules. Resources are treated quite differently from income. The state applies a two-step rule. First, it takes an inventory of all resources owned by *either* spouse. At the option of the couple, this inventory of resources takes place either when you enter the nursing home or when you apply for Medicaid. This inventory will not include the list of excluded resources (e.g., your home, household goods, etc.).

Second, from the total countable resources, Medicaid permits the community spouse to keep a resource allowance that varies by state but must be within a range set by the federal government. States can set the spousal resource allowance as low as $15,804 or as high as $79,020 (for 1997). These figures are adjusted yearly. If the state sets the allowance anywhere below $79,020, then the spouse is entitled to keep the state's allowance *plus* half of any additional assets the couple owns, but no more than $79,020. States and the courts have the authority to increase the spousal allowance in individual cases if the spouse's financial circumstances require.

EXAMPLE OF SPOUSAL ALLOWANCES FOR NURSING HOME CARE

John and Mary are married. John enters a nursing home. They own their house and have savings totaling $120,000. John's income is $1,200 per month and Mary's is $800 per month. The house does not affect eligibility, since Mary lives in it. **Resource allowance:** If the state uses the maximum permissible resource allowance of $79,020, then that figure is her resource allowance (unless she needs a higher allowance because of special needs). But if the state sets the resource allowance at the lowest permissible level for 1997 ($15,804), Mary will be permitted to keep $15,804, plus one-half of the remaining assets. (Since the remaining assets = $104,196, one-half of this is $52,098.) Add these two figures together for her total resource allowance of $67,901. **Monthly income allowance:** Assuming the state uses only the minimum monthly amount permitted ($1,326 in 1997), Mary will be entitled to $526 per month of John's income ($1,326 minus her $800). Depending on her housing costs, Mary might be entitled to some additional allowance from John for excess shelter expenses. John and Mary would benefit from legal help to preserve more of their assets.

THE ROLE OF CHILDREN

Children normally have no legal obligation to pay for their parents' care. In contrast, a spouse may be legally responsible to help pay for the other spouse's care, but it's hard to enforce the responsibility if a spouse is unwilling. If Medicaid enters the picture, the special rules for spousal responsibility described above will apply.

Children often recognize a moral or personal obligation to help pay for a parent's nursing home. A shortage of Medicaid-eligible nursing home beds puts this perception to the test. Some nursing homes admit "private-pay" patients before Medicaid patients, because private-pay rates are higher than what Medicaid pays. Giving priority to private-pay patients is permissible in many states, but illegal in others.

In all states, federal law prohibits nursing homes from requiring payments from families of a resident, or requiring a period of private payment prior to applying for Medicaid coverage. That includes asking for deposits from beneficiaries who are approved for Medicaid but not yet receiving it at the time of admission. Nursing homes cannot obligate an adult child or other third party to guarantee to pay the nursing home's charges. The child's obligation extends only as far as his or her authority over the parent's assets. For example, the child who is an agent under the durable power of attorney of a parent may be obligated *as agent* to pay the nursing home bill out of the parent's assets, but not out of his or her own personal assets. Federal law also prohibits nursing homes from requiring patients to waive or even delay their right to apply to Medicare and/or Medicaid.

MEDICAID ESTATE RECOVERY— PAYING BACK WHAT YOU GET

Federal law requires states to seek recovery of the cost of nursing facility care, home- and community-based services, and related hospital and prescription drug services provided to individuals who were fifty-five or over when they received Medicaid. The home- and community-based services include homemaker services, home health aide services, personal care services, adult day care, respite care, case management, and others. States have the option of recovering for any other Medicaid benefits, in addition to the above, received by a person fifty-five or older. Persons under age fifty-five who are permanent residents of nursing homes may also be subject to recovery under Medicaid.

No recovery can occur from the individual's estate until after the death of the Medicaid beneficiary and the beneficiary's spouse and only if there is no child under age twenty-one, blind, or disabled. What constitutes an estate? At a minimum, **estate** means your **probate estate**—property that passes to others under your will or under the laws of succession in the absence of a will. Property that passes by joint ownership, or insurance contract, life estate, or trust usually stands outside your probate estate. However, states can adopt an expanded definition of "estate" to include this nonprobate property and any other property in which you have any legal title or interest.

Every state must have a procedure to give adequate information about estate recovery to all applicants, provide an appeals process, and establish criteria for waiving recovery in cases of hardship.

Medicaid liens. One way a state can ensure recovery against an estate is to place a lien on the property of the Medicaid beneficiary. A **lien** is a piece of paper filed in the court clerk's office that gives notice that there is a charge against the property. The usual target of the lien is your home. While you are alive, federal law sets certain limits on the use of liens against your home. Liens may be used only to recover for the cost of care of persons *permanently* residing in a nursing home or other medical institution. More important, the state cannot impose the lien if you have a spouse, or child under age twenty-one or blind or disabled, living in the home. In certain cases, the same applies if your brother or sister co-owns the house and lives there.

The rules change somewhat upon your death. In the probate process, the state's claim for recovery of Medicaid benefits may be converted to a lien against your property, including the home, even when one of the above persons still lives there. However, the state may not seek to *enforce* the lien while the surviving spouse is alive or while a child under age twenty-one (or blind or disabled) is living, regardless of whether they are actually living in the house. In addition, the state cannot enforce the lien under limited circumstances if your brother or sister lives there, or if your adult (nondisabled) child lives there if that child was your caregiver under conditions defined by Medicaid.

One way married couples sometimes reduce the impact of the lien and estate recovery provisions is to transfer title of the house to the spouse who remains in the community. Transfers between spouses are permissible under Medicaid. This has the effect of reducing the estate of the spouse in the nursing home. However, do so only with competent legal advice, as there are pitfalls under tax, trust, and estate law.

Nursing home costs can be devastating for a family. Planning ahead can make a big difference. Competent Medicaid planning helps an individual who is unable to pay for long-term care properly meet the Medicaid financial eligibility requirements. Planning may also slow the depletion of your estate or preserve some of it for your spouse or children.

Medicaid planning usually focuses on families who realistically have no other choice but to rely on Medicaid. Few people would opt for Medicaid if other choices were available, because of its disadvantages, including fewer provider choices, limitations in available care, discrimination against Medicaid recipients, and intrusive involvement of the state in your finances and health care. Medicaid planning uses legally permitted options under Medicaid to preserve assets and try to assure you and your dependents some financial security.

Unfortunately, most of the self-help advice regarding Medicaid planning is fraught with danger. Even with competent advice tailored to your needs, Medicaid planning is not easy. The goal here is to introduce you to the types of planning strategies, and not to provide a do-it-yourself program.

Converting assets. "Converting" countable savings into exempt assets is a common strategy. For example, spending $10,000 on needed home improvements converts the cash into exempt equity in your home.

Transfers of assets. Transfers of property for less than **full consideration** (i.e., giving property away in whole or part), *except* for transfers between spouses, can result in a period of ineligibility for Medicaid benefits. When you apply for Medicaid, you must disclose any transfer made within the last thirty-six months (sixty months for certain transfers involving trusts). Such transfers trigger a period of ineligibility that varies from location to location (see example below).

One rule of thumb when transferring property for less than

EXAMPLE OF TRANSFER OF ASSET PENALTY

If Mr. Jones lives in an area where the average monthly cost of nursing home care is $3,000 per month, and he gives away $90,000 on January 1, 1997, he is disqualified from Medicaid until July 1, 1999 (i.e., 30 months). This is calculated as follows: $90,000 ÷ $3,000 = 30 months (or two years, six months). Thus, he must wait at least thirty months to apply for Medicaid in order to avoid the penalty.

full consideration, for purposes of Medicaid planning, is to retain enough assets to be able to pay for nursing home care for the duration of the penalty period. However, this is only a generalization. Every situation is different.

Use of trusts. Irrevocable trusts are another planning tool to help manage the cost of long-term care. Trusts that can be revoked by the creator of the trust are always considered countable assets by Medicaid and do not help establish Medicaid eligibility. However, irrevocable trusts, if created at least *sixty months* prior to applying for Medicaid (the "look-back" period for trusts), may help establish Medicaid eligibility while slowing down the depeletion of your estate, but the discretion of the trustee to distribute income and principal must be sharply limited. Federal law permits certain trusts created for the benefit of persons with disability under sixty-five. Generally, parents who are planning for the long-term care of an adult disabled child may want to consider this type of trust.

An irrevocable **Miller trust** (named after a legal case) is relevant to persons living in "income cap" states (see page 79). The problem faced by some persons in these states is that their income may be just over the Medicaid income cap but less than the amount needed to pay privately for a nursing home bed. To remedy this hardship, federal law requires these states to exempt (for purposes of Medicaid eligibility) trusts created for their benefit, if the trust is composed only of pension, Social Security, or other income, and if at the individual's death the state is reimbursed by the trust for all Medicaid assistance paid on behalf of the individual. These trusts work by paying out a monthly income just under the Medicaid cap and retaining the rest. The result is that most of the individual's income, supplemented by Medicaid, goes toward payment of the nursing home. The remainder of the person's income stays in the trust until his or her death. The accumulated residue is then paid to Medicaid.

Other limited trust arrangements may be helpful in some cases, but they all require careful assessment and advice and a good dose of caution. Remember that Congress periodically changes the rules, so your planning may have to change accordingly.

PRIVATE LONG-TERM-CARE INSURANCE

Long-term-care insurance helps pay for nursing home care, home care, and sometimes other services for an extended period of time—two or more years. Long-term-care insurance is still relatively new, so its features continue to change yearly. Most individual policies can be purchased only by persons between fifty and eighty-four, and a medical screening is typically required. Not every older person needs or can afford a long-term-care insurance policy. They're best for those with income and assets to protect, and those who can afford this form of protection against the potential costs of long-term care.

Most long-term-care policies pay a preset amount for each day of covered nursing home care or home health care, or sometimes a per-visit amount for home care.

Examine specific provisions carefully before purchasing

one, since the conditions and limitations on coverage can be extensive and complex. The most comprehensive policies cover all levels of nursing home care—skilled, intermediate, and custodial care—plus "assisted living" facilities. **Assisted living facilities** provide a level of support less than nursing home care and may be a better alternative for people who can no longer live at home. Likewise, better policies will cover **home care,** broadly defined to include not only skilled home health services, but also some range of nonmedical, supportive services such as homemaker, home health aide, or personal care services. Newer policies even offer coverage options such as adult day care for the individual or respite care for the family.

Costs. The costs depend on your age at the time of purchase, the extent of coverage, and your health history. Age is clearly the single greatest factor. The annual premium for a seventy-five-year-old can be double or triple that for a sixty-five-year-old. Annual costs for a policy that includes both nursing home and home care coverage may range as high as $1,500 for a person fifty-five at the time of purchase, $2,600 for a sixty-five-year-old, and $5,000 for a seventy-five-year-old.

EVALUATING A LONG-TERM-CARE POLICY

Compare more than one policy side by side. Your state's insurance department should have names of companies offering long-term-care insurance. Most states have begun to set minimum standards and consumer protection guidelines. Guides for evaluating policies may also be available from your state insurance department or your office on aging.

Keep in mind the following tips:

1. Pick reputable companies first. Be sure that the company will be around and solvent for a long time.

2. Make sure your policy will pay benefits for all levels of care in a nursing home, including custodial care, as well as assisted living facilities or residential care facilities.
3. A good policy will pay benefits for home care, including in-home personal care to help with activities of daily living.
4. Consider whether the amount of daily benefits will be adequate in the future. Consider only policies with an "inflation adjuster" that increases benefits by a certain percentage each year to keep pace with inflation. The cost of long-term care has consistently increased faster than cost-of-living indicators.
5. Do not assume that more years of coverage are always better. For example, few people ever need nursing home care for five years. Moreover, keep in mind the amount of assets you have to protect. Even with long-term-care insurance, you may deplete your assets over time. If your policy continues to pay benefits even after your remaining resources are gone, the policy may serve only to reduce the state's payments under Medicaid, rather than your costs.
6. Six months is considered a reasonable exclusion period for pre-existing conditions.
7. Better policies will allow payment of nursing home or home health benefits without requiring a prior period of hospitalization as a condition of coverage.
8. Most policies impose waiting periods that restrict the starting time of benefits after you begin receiving nursing home care or home care—twenty to ninety days is a common waiting period. A longer waiting period will lower the premium cost. First-day coverage will increase your premium.
9. Avoid policies that pay only for "medically necessary" care. That standard is too discretionary. Most good policies cover help with activities of daily living and, alternatively, cognitive impairment. Be sure your policy covers Alzheimer's disease and other forms of dementia. About half the residents of nursing home suffer some form of dementia.
10. Be sure that the premium remains constant over the life of the policy and that the policy is guaranteed renewable for life.
11. Buy a policy only from a company that is licensed in your state

and has agents physically present in your state. Out-of-state mail-order policies may leave you powerless to remedy problems if anything goes wrong.

FINAL QUESTION: HOW MUCH INSURANCE DO I REALLY NEED?

The best recommendation for anyone on Medicare, who is not also on Medicaid, is to purchase one good Medigap policy and one long-term-care insurance policy if you have assets you want to protect and can reasonably afford it.

WHERE TO GET MORE INFORMATION AND HELP

MEDICAID AND LONG-TERM CARE

- The **Health Care Financing Administration (HCFA)** publishes a variety of helpful material about Medicaid. Social Security offices will carry some of it, but the most up-to-date and complete resource is HCFA's web page on the Internet: http://www.hcfa.gov.

- Medicaid differs from state to state. To find out what information is available about Medicaid in your state, contact your state or local area agency on aging. Find them in your telephone book or call the **National Eldercare Locator** at (800) 677-1116. You can also search the database of the National Eldercare Locator on-line through their web page at http://www.ageinfo.org/elderloc.

- *Long-Term Care Planning: A Dollar & Sense Guide,* by **United Seniors Health Cooperative**, 1331 H Street, NW, Suite 500, Washington, DC 20005-4706. This guide covers various resources available inside your family and in your community, including Medicare, Medicaid, and long-term-care insurance. Also published by United Seniors is *Long-Term-Care Insurance: To Buy or Not to Buy?*, a concise guide to long-term-care insurance. Call (202) 393-6222, or visit their website at http://www.ushc-online.org.

- *The Consumer's Guide to Long-Term-Care Insurance*, by the **Health Insurance Association of America**, 1025 Connecticut Avenue, NW, Washington, DC 20036-3998, provides useful guidance and a checklist for comparing policies. Their toll-free consumer help line is (800) 942-4242. This publication and other useful consumer information are also available on their web page on the Internet: http://www.hiaa.org.

CHAPTER FIVE

Housing and Long-Term-Care Choices

THE RANGE OF HOUSING OPTIONS for older people is enormous—from staying in your own home, to sharing a home, to moving into housing designed for seniors. Where you live may depend on your health needs, your relationship to your family, your financial situation, and your ties to your current community. A continuum of housing arrangements is illustrated on page 98. This chapter takes a look at all these options with an eye on protecting your rights and ensuring that your individual needs are met.

Getting older does not necessarily mean losing your independence. However, many people begin to need some assistance as they age. You may choose supportive services that are available through agencies in the community, such as the area agency on aging. Or you may decide to move to housing where services are provided. No matter where you live, be a careful consumer—be aware of risks and benefits, and your legal rights.

OPTIONS FOR HOMEOWNERS

If you own your home, and need assistance or services, or if your home needs repairs or modifications, check with your local area agency on aging about help available in your community.

Reverse mortgages and other loans allow you to borrow against your home equity without having to repay the money until some future time. These loans have pros and cons, and raise a number of legal issues.

REVERSE MORTGAGES

A **reverse mortgage** lets you borrow against the equity in your home, without having to repay the loan right away. You can get the money in a lump sum, in monthly cash payments for life, or by drawing on a line of credit, or you can choose a combination of these options (e.g., monthly payments plus a line of credit for emergencies). The amount you can borrow and the size of the loan installments are based on several factors, including: your age, the value of the home and of the equity you hold, the interest rate, and the kind of loan you select. These loans can be costly, but the relative costs lessen over time, and you will never owe more than the value of your home.

Most reverse mortgages have no restrictions on how you use the money. The loan usually does not have to be repaid until you sell, move from your home, or die, although some

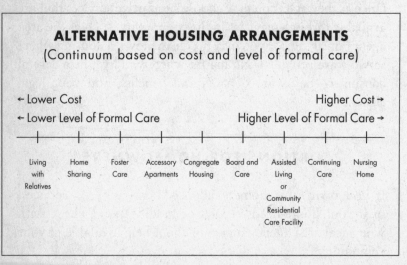

ALTERNATIVE HOUSING ARRANGEMENTS

(Continuum based on cost and level of formal care)

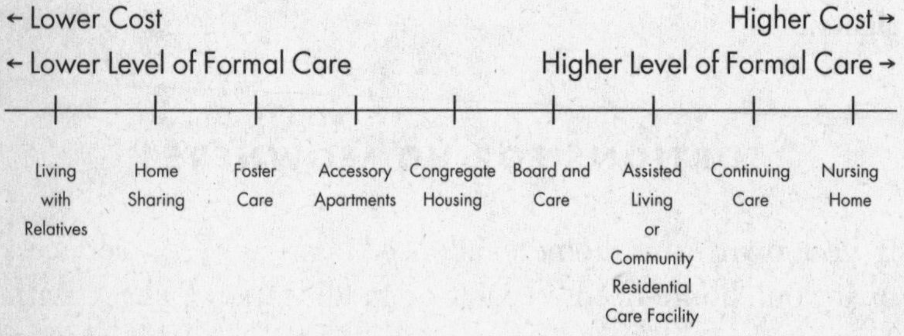

loans must be repaid at the end of a specified number of years. Some lenders combine a reverse mortgage with an annuity that allows you to receive loan payments under the annuity even after you sell your home and move.

When you sell your home or move, or at the end of the term, you must repay the money you have borrowed plus the accrued interest and fees. The house can be sold to repay the loan, or the funds collected some other way. The lender is not permitted to collect more than the appraised value of the house at the time the loan is repaid, even if the loan exceeds that amount.

The most widely available product is the federally insured **Home Equity Conversion Mortgage (HECM)**. Under this program, the Federal Housing Authority (FHA) provides insurance for reverse mortgages placed through private financial institutions. Another reverse mortgage program available nationally through private lenders is **Home Keeper Mortgage,** backed by Fannie Mae (the Federal National Mortgage Association). A few private companies also offer their own reverse mortgage products. These tend to be more costly, because the lender must charge customers more in order to self-insure against potential losses. Federal law requires all reverse mortgage lenders to inform you, before making the loan, of the total amount you will owe through the course of the loan. This enables you to compare costs.

Eligibility. Eligibility depends on the individual product, but most have rules similar to the FHA and Fannie Mae programs. The borrower and every other person whose name is on the deed must:

- be at least sixty-two and
- own the property free and clear, except for liens or mortgages that can be paid off with proceeds from the loan.

In addition, the property must be:

- the borrower's primary residence (that is, not a vacation home);
- a single-family residence (condominiums are available under the FHA program but not the Fannie Mae; at this time, mobile homes and cooperatives are not eligible).

Will a reverse mortgage affect my Social Security? Income from a reverse mortgage will not affect your eligibility for Social Security, Medicare, or other retirement benefits, or for pensions that are not based on need.

What about other government benefits? Unless you plan carefully, reverse mortgage payments may affect your eligibility for Supplemental Security Income (SSI), Medicaid, food stamps, and some state benefit programs. These benefits are designed to meet basic needs, and recipients must meet strict financial guidelines.

The general rule is that reverse mortgage payments will *not* affect your eligibility for benefits if you spend the money during the month in which it is received. But if you do not spend that money during that month, it will be counted as a resource. If your resources are greater than the allowable limit, your benefits could be reduced or eliminated. Some state benefit programs follow the federal rules on this issue, but it is most important to check the rules in your own state.

Federal eligibility rules for **reverse *annuity* mortgages,** under which you receive payments even after you move from your home, raise tax and benefits issues different from regular reverse mortgages. Reverse annuity mortgage payments are counted as income for purposes of SSI, Medicaid, and similar need-based benefits, even if they are spent in the month in which they are received. They will reduce benefits, and may affect your eligibility altogether. Annuities also receive less favorable tax treatment than do loan advances.

Tax consequences.

- Are reverse mortgage payments taxed? So far, the IRS has not taxed reverse mortgage payments, on the ground that the money is a loan. However, a portion of reverse annuity payments will be taxed.
- Is the interest deductible? The general rule is that interest cannot be deducted until it is actually paid. Since you do not pay the interest on a reverse mortgage until the loan comes due, it most likely will not be deductible until that time.

Reverse mortgages may also have an effect on estate taxes. Consult a tax adviser.

Estate planning considerations. Reverse mortgages allow you to spend your home equity while you are alive. You may end up using all of your equity, and not have any left to pass down to your heirs. Some plans allow you to set aside some of the equity, so that it is not used.

Reverse mortgage counseling. The HECM requires all potential borrowers to receive counseling from an agency certified by the U.S. Department of Housing and Urban Development. Some state laws require counseling for all borrowers, no matter what the product, but borrowers looking at private products generally are not required to have counseling.

Reverse mortgages are very complex and involve difficult financial, legal, and personal decisions. Examine them carefully, and look for alternatives that may suit your needs. Talk to a lawyer who is familiar with the issues, and discuss your aims and concerns with family.

SELLING WITHOUT MOVING

You can also put your home equity to practical use with sale-leasebacks, life estates, and charitable annuities. Each of these options has significant consequences and should be used only with professional guidance.

Sale-leasebacks. In a sale-leaseback, you sell your home, but retain the right to live there paying rent. The buyer usually makes a substantial down payment to you. You act as a lender by giving the buyer a mortgage. You get the buyer's mortgage payments; the buyer gets your rent payments. You remain in the home, and can use the down payment and the mortgage payments as income. The buyer can deduct the mortgage interest payment from his or her income, and will also benefit if the value of the property increases.

However, the IRS requires that both the sale price and the rental payments be fair market rate. Sale-leasebacks used to be good investments, especially for adult children, but today there are fewer tax advantages, so finding an investor may be difficult.

Life estates. In a life estate, or **sale of a remainder interest plan,** you sell your home but retain the right to live there during your lifetime. The buyer pays you a lump sum, or monthly payments, or both. You are usually responsible for taxes and repairs while you live in the house. At your death, full ownership passes automatically to the buyer. This arrangement is used most commonly within families, as part of an estate plan. As with a sale-leaseback, it might be difficult to find an outside investor.

Charitable remainder trusts. In a charitable remainder trust, you donate your home to a charitable institution in return for a lifetime annuity and possibly a tax deduction. You retain a life estate, and you remain responsible for taxes and maintenance. When you die, your home becomes the property of the charitable institution.

REGULAR HOME EQUITY LOANS

A traditional home equity loan is very different from a reverse mortgage, and can be risky for an older person on a fixed income. As with a reverse mortgage, you borrow against the equity you have built up in your home. But in a home equity loan, you must make regular monthly payments or you may lose your home.

Home equity loans do have tax advantages. It is no longer possible to deduct interest on consumer goods such as car loans and credit card bills. But with home equity loans, you can borrow up to $100,000 on the equity in your first and second home, use the money for any purpose, and deduct the interest you pay on the loan. You can deduct the interest on a home equity loan that exceeds $100,000 if you use the money for home improvements.

ALTERNATIVE BENEFITS FOR HOMEOWNERS

Before deciding on a reverse mortgage or other home equity conversion plan, explore other ways to increase your income. You may be eligible for government benefits, such as Supplemental Security Income or Medicaid (see chapters 2 and 4 for further discussion).

Some states sponsor **property tax credit** or **deferral programs** that give older homeowners a tax break by reducing taxes, or delaying payment until the house is sold, or freezing the tax rate when you reach a certain age.

If your house is in need of repairs, or if you need to do some minor renovations to accommodate a disability (e.g., build a ramp, widen a doorway, or install grab bars in the bathroom), the state may have a **home repair program** that provides funds to help you.

Another option is **accessory housing,** which helps you create private rental units in, or next to, a single-family home (your home or another's). Finally, your city or county may also sponsor a **home-sharing program,** in which homeowners are matched with individuals seeking housing in exchange for rent or services.

To find out more about these programs, call your local agency on aging.

OPTIONS FOR APARTMENT DWELLERS

There are a number of different kinds of apartments for older people, including federally assisted apartments, public housing, and private sector housing. Apartment living frees you from repairs and other responsibilities, but you may not be permitted to keep a pet, or you may have to get permission to redecorate or remodel.

Congregate care refers to complexes with separate apartments (including kitchens) and some housekeeping services and usually one or more daily group meals available. Many congregate care facilities are subsidized under federal housing programs. Personal care and health oversight are usually not part of the facility's services, although they may be provided through community social services. Some federally assisted apartment buildings provide supportive services (help with necessary activities like housekeeping or personal hygiene), and some have a service coordinator on the premises. Most residents of privately owned buildings must make their own arrangements.

If you have a disability, you have special legal rights (see chapter 6).

OTHER RETIREMENT HOUSING CHOICES

SUPPORTIVE HOUSING

In the past few years, public and private housing options for older people have increased. These options vary from single-family homes that offer board and care to large institutional complexes. They share one common characteristic in providing some combination of housing and supportive services. Supportive services may consist of:

- help with **activities of daily living (ADLs)**—such as eating, dressing, transferring from one position to another (e.g., sitting to standing), using a toilet, and bathing;
- help with **instrumental activities of daily living (IADLs)**—such as preparing meals, taking medications, walking outside, using the telephone, managing money, shopping, and housekeeping;
- **protective oversight**—monitoring, reminding, or other supervision, particularly for someone with cognitive impairment.

The three most common types of supportive housing are board and care homes, assisted living facilities, and continuing care retirement communities.

Board and care facilities are group residences that provide room, board, twenty-four-hour protective oversight, and assistance with some ADLs and IADLs. They generally do not provide any medical services, although some assist with medications. Facilities may have as few as two residents or as many as two hundred. Other names for board and care include: residential care facility, domiciliary care, homes for the aged, community-based residential facility, or assisted living facility.

Assisted living facilities offer the same services. However, they tend to be more "upscale," usually providing small apartments (often with kitchen facilities) or more private rooms and baths, plus more social and recreational opportunities, and a more individualized approach to care. They also place more emphasis on encouraging independence, autonomy, privacy, and the right to make choices in a homelike setting.

Continuing care retirement communities (CCRCs) offer a broader level of care. Living options range from independent living apartments, to assisted living (either in your apartment or in an assisted living wing or unit), to skilled nursing home care. Most CCRCs also require a substantial entrance fee as well as monthly fees, although some charge only monthly fees. A few CCRCs allow you to buy an ownership interest in your living unit (in a condo or co-op) with a personal and health services package included. These ownership arrangements are complex and pose both special advantages and risks.

One type of CCRC, the **life care facility,** has virtually disappeared. Under these arrangements, residents turned over all their assets or paid the total lifetime fee in advance in return for shelter, health care, and supportive services for life. These types of contracts went the way of the dinosaur, because the assets and fees were not sufficient to keep up with rising health care expenses.

CCRCs may be privately owned, government-supported, or sponsored by nonprofit organizations. CCRCs are, along with nursing homes, at the other end of the continuum on housing from independent living (see page 98). How CCRCs are specifically defined varies from state to state, and sometimes even within states. State law protections vary substantially, too.

What to look for in a CCRC or assisted living community. Entering any kind of retirement community is a major commitment.

RETIREMENT HOUSING BY ANY OTHER NAME . . .

Housing programs for older persons have many names. But for the consumer, the questions are the same. What will your living conditions be, how much will it cost, what will you get for your money, will the programs meet your health and safety needs, who will be making the decisions, and how much independence will you have?

Consider the decision carefully and seek professional advice from a lawyer or financial adviser before you make a commitment. If you change your mind, you may not be able to get your money back.

Don't rely on advertisements.

- Visit the facility at length and talk to both staff and residents.
- Check with the state office on aging to find out whether the facility is regulated, and see whether there have been any problems with it.
- Ask for a copy of the contract, read it carefully, and have it reviewed by a lawyer.

CHECKLIST OF QUESTIONS FOR ASSISTED LIVING AND CONTINUING CARE

These questions will help you to evaluate and compare just about any kind of supportive housing arrangement.

QUESTIONS REGARDING THE SOLVENCY AND EXPERTISE OF THE PROVIDER

1. *What is the provider's background and experience?* The provider is the person or entity legally and financially responsible for providing the housing. Some facilities advertise that they are "sponsored" by nonprofit groups or churches that in reality have no legal control or financial responsibility. Be wary if such illusory sponsorship is trumpeted.
2. *Is the provider financially sound?* Ask a professional to review the facility's financial, actuarial, and operating statements. Does it have sufficient financial reserves?
3. *Are all levels of care licensed or certified by the state?* Check with the state office on aging and with the state licensing agency.
4. *How does the facility ensure the quality of its care and services? Is it accredited by any recognized private accrediting organization?*

QUESTIONS REGARDING FEES AND ACCOMMODATIONS

5. *If there is an entrance fee, how much is it, and can you get a refund of all or part of it?* The facility should provide a formula for a pro rata refund, based on the resident's length of stay, regardless of whether the facility or the resident initiates the termination. Some facilities offer fully refundable entrance fees.
6. *What is the monthly fee? When and how much can it be increased? What happens if you cannot afford higher fees?* Some facilities give residents financial help if they become unable to pay.
7. *Do the fees change when the resident's living arrangements or level-of-care needs change?*
8. *How much say do you have in choosing where you live? How large is the living unit? Can you change or redecorate it?*
9. *What if your marital status changes? Will your payments change, or will you be asked to move, if you marry, divorce, become widowed, or have a friend or family member move into the unit?*
10. *What if spouses require different levels of care?*

QUESTIONS REGARDING SERVICES AND HEALTH CARE

11. *What services are included in my regular fees?* Ask about coverage, limitations (based on cost, time, or number of visits), and special charges for the following matters:

Supportive/Social/Recreational Services

- Meal services: Is the schedule reasonable? Is it flexible?
- Special diets/tray service: e.g., What is the policy on eating in your room?
- Utilities: Are they included in the monthly fee?
- Cable television: Is it available? Who pays?
- Furnishings: Can you bring your own?

- Unit maintenance: Who is responsible for repairs?
- Linens/personal laundry: Is there an extra charge for laundry?
- Housekeeping: Is it included in the fees? What are the options?
- Recreational/cultural activities: What is available? What is on-site?
- Transportation: To where? Is there a limit on the number of trips?
- Safety: What kind of security system and policies are in place? Is there a fire emergency plan?

Health and Personal Care

- Assessment and plan of care: What kind of assessment is done to determine your needs and a plan for meeting those needs? What are the qualifications of the person doing the assessment? Is a detailed plan of care developed? When and how is it reviewed?
- Physician services: Can you choose your own doctor?
- Medications: Who gives medications? How is it coordinated with your physician?
- Nursing care facility services: Are they on-site? Who pays?
- Nursing services outside a nursing unit: Is assistance with medications provided?
- Private duty nursing: Is it available? Are there limits?
- Dental and eye care: Is it included in fees? Available on-site?
- Personal care services: What if you need assistance with eating, dressing, bathing, toileting, etc.?
- Homemaker/companion services: Are they available? Is there a limit?

- Drugs, medication, and medical equipment/supplies: Who pays?
- Emergency call system: Is it available? Who pays?

12. *Are additional services always guaranteed? If the facility provides a nursing unit, what happens if a bed is not available when you need it?*
13. *Can services be changed? To what extent does the facility have the right to cut back, change, or eliminate services, or change the fees?*
14. *What about preexisting conditions? Does the facility limit its responsibility for certain health conditions or preexisting conditions? Can the facility ask you to move if you become too sick or impaired to be cared for by the facility?*
15. *Who pays for health care? Can you receive Medicare and Medicaid coverage in the facility? Does the facility require residents to buy private insurance or participate in a special group insurance program for residents?*
16. *Who decides that you need more care, and on what grounds? What are the criteria and procedures for determining when a resident needs to be transferred from independent living to assisted living, or to a nursing care unit, or to an entirely different facility? Who is involved in these decisions?*
17. *What are the staffing levels? What are the professional qualifications of the staff?* Nursing homes are regulated, but assisted living and other supervised care may not be. Make sure that staff is professionally equipped to do their jobs. What kind of emergencies are staff expected to handle and how are they trained for them?

QUESTIONS REGARDING THE RIGHTS OF RESIDENTS

18. *Can residents participate in facility management and decision making? What input do you have in activity and meal planning and in house rules? Is there a resident council? How are complaints and disputes handled?*

19. *What if you want an exception to a policy or to routine scheduling?*
20. *What are the grounds for eviction? Is there a right to appeal?*
21. *Are the general operating rules reasonable? What rules cover the facility's day-to-day operation? Are they reasonable? What happens if you break a rule? Can you appeal?*
22. *What happens if you are injured? Does the contract release the facility from liability for injury resulting from negligence?* Avoid such waivers.

NURSING HOME CARE

What are your legal rights as a resident of a nursing home? What should you consider when looking for a nursing home? What can you do when problems arise with the quality of care? This section answers these and other questions.

CCRC INDUSTRY PROFILED

A recent study by the American Association of Homes and Services for the Aging shows that:

- Five states are home to nearly 40 percent of CCRCs (Pennsylvania, California, Florida, Illinois, and Ohio).
- More than 350,000 older adults live in CCRCs.
- For a one-bedroom unit, the average low entry fee is $59,000 and the average high entry fee is $85,868; the average low monthly fee for a one-bedroom unit is $1,046 and the average high monthly fee is $1,399.

Source: David W. Scruggs, *Dare to Discover the Future of Continuing Care Retirement Communities.* Washington, D.C.: American Association of Homes and Services for the Aging, 1995.

When you are faced with the possibility of nursing home placement, be sure to read up on the alternatives to nursing home care described throughout this chapter. Alternatives, in the form of home- and community-based care and assisted living, are becoming more available every day.

THE NURSING HOME INDUSTRY

Nursing homes are big business. Seventy percent of the 16,000 homes in the United States are for-profit businesses, and many are large multistate chains. All nursing facilities must be licensed under state law, and more than 80 percent choose to participate in Medicare and Medicaid, which require them to meet federal certification standards on quality of care, quality of life, and residents' rights. Unfortunately, monitoring and enforcing of those standards vary substantially from place to place. There are good facilities out there, but no easy way to identify them.

Technically, a nursing facility provides skilled nursing and medical care; rehabilitation services for injured, disabled, or sick persons; other health-related services; and custodial care. **Custodial care** refers to help with eating, dressing, bathing, toileting, and moving about. Medicare does not pay for custodial nursing care. Chapters 3 and 4 describe the payment systems that cover nursing home care.

FINDING A NURSING HOME

Many nursing home admissions happen under stress. Even when you have time for deliberation, choosing a good nursing home is difficult, because there are limited sources of information about how facilities compare.

In hospitals, "discharge planners," who are usually social

workers, can help. They have general information about the facilities in your area, but they probably don't know about the actual quality of care in facilities. Guides on selecting a nursing home will not give you quick or simple answers, either. State and local nursing home ombudsmen, described below, are probably the best source of information. They visit facilities and respond to complaints from nursing home residents and families, so they get a sense of strengths and weaknesses. However, they may not be willing to share their opinions, for fear of being accused of bias.

As a starting point, you can obtain a facility's inspection report. States usually inspect homes once a year. The reports detail major and minor deficiencies. Virtually every facility, even the very best, will have some problems. The job of caring for highly impaired individuals is difficult. Be wary of facilities that have serious deficiencies or that repeatedly have the same problems (such as in giving medication, prevalence of incontinence or bed sores, or using restraints). Compare the last three or four inspections. If the same problems never get resolved, then even minor deficiencies become major shortcomings. Nursing homes are required to have their inspection reports available for you to read. If the home does not have it, or makes it difficult to examine, consider that a serious "red flag," indicating quality problems. State nursing home licensing agencies—usually part of the state health department—can also make the report available to you, and often state or local ombudsman programs will also have them.

Visit the facility you are considering on more than one occasion at different times of day. Observe mealtimes, resident activities, and the interaction between staff and residents. Be wary of administrators who make access difficult or evade your questions. Look for both positive and negative signs of quality care, such as the following:

	Signs of Good Quality	Signs of Poor Quality
Staff	Numerous staff interact personally with residents in a friendly and respectful manner.	Few staff are on duty, do not interact with residents, or do so in an impersonal or brusque manner.
Food/ Mealtimes	The food is appetizing to you and served in a dining room that encourages people to socialize. Staff are available to help residents who need assistance. Residents needing help are integrated with other residents.	Food is unappetizing/cold and served in setting that does not encourage socializing. Staff are not available to give assistance. Residents needing assistance are fed elsewhere or at a different time.
Building Appearance	The most important rooms are residents' rooms. They should be personalized and homey.	Resident rooms are drab, look institutionalized. Indicates residents are not encouraged to personalize their rooms.
Resident Appearance	Residents are reasonably well groomed, clean, and appropriately dressed.	Residents are inappropriately dressed, dirty, or unkempt. Indicates inadequate staffing.
Restraints	Few, and preferably no, residents are restrained, physically or by medication. Ask the administrator how many are restrained.	Many residents are in restraints, or facility cannot give you a clear answer. Indicates inadequate care or inadequate staffing.
Bedsores	Preferably no residents suffer from bedsores, but you probably cannot tell from a brief visit. Check recent state	Bedsores are more than a rare occurrence, or facility cannot give you a straight answer. Indicates inadequate care

	Signs of Good Quality	Signs of Poor Quality
	inspection reports and ask the administrator for numbers.	planning or inadequate staffing.
Smells	Facility is generally free of offensive odors.	Lingering, offensive odors throughout building. Indicates inadequate staffing to clean up accidents.
Activities	Substantial numbers of residents enjoy frequently scheduled activities.	The activity calendar is pretty empty or uncreative in its offerings. Most residents are sitting around in dayrooms doing nothing.

RESIDENTS' RIGHTS

You do not surrender your rights and privileges when you enter a nursing home. Although institutional care limits your lifestyle and privacy, you should nevertheless expect high-quality, compassionate, and dignified care.

The federal **Nursing Home Reform Amendments of 1987,** and corresponding state laws, protect residents. For residents who lack decision-making capacity, the resident's agent under a power of attorney for health care or another legal surrogate recognized by state law (typically a family member) may exercise the resident's rights.

Federal law requires that nursing homes meet strong basic standards for both the **quality of life** and the **quality of care** of each resident. The home must provide services and activities to attain or maintain the highest practicable physical, mental, and psychosocial well-being of each resident. This is done through a required resident assessment and a written **plan of care,** which is prepared with the resident or the resident's family or legal representative. This process should occur just after admission and then yearly or after any significant change in physical or mental condition.

The law also guarantees the following specific rights:

Information rights. The nursing home must provide:

- written information about your rights;
- written information about the services included under their monthly fee rate and any extra charges for additional services;
- advance notice of any changes in room assignment or roommate;
- an explanation of your right to make a health care advance directive and information about their policies on complying with advance directives (see discussion of advance directives in chapter 9);
- information about eligibility for Medicare and Medicaid and the services covered by those programs.

Self-determination rights. Each resident has the right to:

- participate in an individualized assessment and a care-planning process that accommodates the resident's personal needs and preferences;
- choose a personal physician;
- voice complaints without fear of reprisal, and to receive a prompt response;
- organize and participate in resident groups (such as a resident council) and family groups.

Personal and privacy rights. Residents have the right to:

- participate in social, religious, and community activities however they choose;
- privacy in medical treatment, accommodations, personal visits, written and telephone communications and meetings of resident and family groups;

- confidentiality in the use of all personal and clinical records;
- access to long-term-care ombudsmen, their physicians, family members, and reasonable access to other visitors;
- freedom from physical or mental abuse, corporal punishment, and involuntary seclusion;
- freedom from any physical restraint or psychoactive drug used for purposes of convenience or discipline, and not required to treat medical symptoms;
- protection of resident's funds held by the facility, including the right to a quarterly accounting.

Transfer and discharge rights. A resident may be transferred or discharged only for the following reasons:

- The health, safety, or welfare of the resident requires it.
- The health, safety, or welfare of other residents requires it.
- Nonpayment of fees.
- The resident's health improves so that he or she no longer needs nursing home care.
- The facility closes.

Normally, residents must receive at least thirty days' advance notice, with information about how to appeal any transfer or discharge decision and how to contact the state long-term-care ombudsman program. The facility also must provide adequate discharge planning to prepare and orient residents for a safe and orderly transfer from the facility.

Protection against Medicaid discrimination. Nursing homes that participate in the Medicaid program must:

- have identical policies and practices regarding services to residents regardless of the source of payment—in other words, basic care and services must be the same for Medicaid residents as for private-pay residents (but remember that not all facilities participate in Medicaid);

- provide you with information on how to apply for Medicaid;
- explain the Medicaid "bed-hold" policy—that is, how many days Medicaid will hold the resident's bed or give priority readmission after a hospitalization or other absence;
- not require, request, or encourage residents to waive their rights to Medicaid;
- not require a family member to guarantee payment (i.e., be personally financially liable);
- not charge, solicit, accept, or receive gifts, money, donations, or other valuable consideration as a precondition for admission or continued stay under Medicaid.

WHAT TO DO WHEN PROBLEMS ARISE

Different problems require different responses. Try these steps when problems arise. The order may vary depending on the problem.

1. Keep a written log of the relevant details (when? where? who? what? why?).
2. Try to resolve the problem informally by talking to the supervising nurse, social worker, or administrator.
3. If the resident's needs have changed or the care plan is inadequate, you have a right to a new assessment and care-planning conference. This should result in an individually tailored plan of care.
4. Bring the problem to the attention of the resident council or family council. Better facilities have active councils of this sort.
5. Contact your long-term-care ombudsman.
6. Contact the state agency that licenses nursing homes. Usually, the state department of health has this responsibility.
7. Contact a community legal assistance program or other advo-

cacy organization. For problems involving serious physical, mental, or emotional harm, consult an attorney experienced in long-term-care issues.

The long-term-care ombudsman program. The federal **Older Americans Act** requires every state to operate a long-term-care ombudsman program. The ombudsman is responsible for advocating on behalf of nursing home residents and residents of other long-term-care facilities. The ombudsman can provide information about options and rights, and can resolve complaints.

Most states have local or regional programs. Ombudsman staff can be effective partners in resolving problems. Federal law requires nursing homes to allow the ombudsman access to residents and facilities. In addition, the ombudsman usually has special authority under state law to inspect records and take other steps necessary to respond to complaints.

HOME- AND COMMUNITY-BASED CARE AND SERVICES

In your state or locale, you will probably find programs designed to meet the daily needs of older adults and to enable them to "age in place"—at home and in the community. Some charge fees, but others are subsidized by tax dollars or private nonprofit agencies.

Agencies on aging play a central role. Each state has a unit on aging, in charge of a comprehensive service system. Most state agencies are divided into a number of smaller **area agencies on aging**. These area agencies, or "Triple A's," may be located within county government, regional planning councils, units of city government, or private nonprofit organizations. They plan services for older persons, coordinate the delivery system, and advocate for the elderly. Most area agencies on aging do not deliver services directly, but contract with local providers for social services, such as those listed below. Together, the state and area agencies on aging, service providers, and advocates are known as the **aging network**.

TYPICAL HOME- AND COMMUNITY-BASED SERVICES

transportation
outreach
information and referral
case management
home health care
protective services
employment services
counseling
volunteer programs
residential repair
crime prevention/victim
money management
senior centers
legal assistance
housing services
respite care
personal care services
homemaker services
chore services
home-delivered meals
congregate meal programs
friendly visitors
adult day care
other supportive services

FINDING SERVICES THAT MIGHT HELP

Start by calling your local or state agency on aging. You can find the number in your phone book or by calling the national Eldercare Locator at (800) 677-1116, which can also identify other community resources. Most agencies on aging have written materials that describe resources available in the community or through state or national organizations. Some have brochures that identify common problems the elderly face and ways to solve particular problems. The agency on aging in your community is usually the best starting point for any questions about aging services, rights, and opportunities.

WHERE TO GET MORE INFORMATION AND HELP

HOMEOWNERS' OPTIONS

- The **American Association of Retired Persons (AARP)** provides valuable consumer information on home equity conversion options:
  - *Home-Made Money.* A guide that provides valuable help in understanding reverse mortgage options, including FHA-insured reverse mortgages.
  - *Reverse Mortgage Lenders List.* State-by-state list of financial institutions offering federally insured reverse mortgages, updated quarterly. Available on-line at the AARP's website.

  Contact AARP, 601 E Street, NW, Washington, DC 20049; (202) 434-2277 or (800) 424-3410, or visit their home page on the World Wide Web at http://www.aarp.org.

- *Retirement Income on the House* (1992) and *Your New Retirement Nest Egg* (1995), two comprehensive consumer guides by Ken Scholen of the **National Center for Home Equity Conversion**, Suite 115, 7373 147th Street West, Apple Valley, MN 55124. (These titles may also be in your local library or bookstore.)
- For more information on the Home Keeper Mortgage described in this chapter, and a list of participating lenders, call Fannie Mae at (800) 732-6643, or write to: **Fannie Mae Public Information Office**, 3900 Wisconsin Avenue, NW, Washington, DC 20016-2899. Fannie Mae's home page on the World Wide Web is http://www.fanniemae.com.

ASSISTED LIVING AND CCRCs

- The **American Association of Homes and Services for the Aging (AAHSA)** publishes *The Consumer's Directory of Continuing Care Retirement Communities,* profiling not-for-profit retirement communities around the country and providing an overview of CCRC types, terminology, and features. For ordering information, contact AAHSA Publications, Dept. 5119, Washington, DC 20061-5119; (301) 490-0677 or (800) 508-9442. AASHA's home page on the World Wide Web is http://www.aahsa.org.

- **AARP** has several consumer publications about assisted living and continuing care communities, including:

  - *Housing Options for Older Americans*
  - *Selecting Retirement Housing*
  - *Staying at Home*
  - *Retirement Housing: Bibliography of Housing from AARP*

  Contact information for AARP is listed above.

- State or local agencies on aging frequently prepare guides to housing options. Find the agency's number in your local telephone book.

NURSING HOMES

- By far the most indispensable consumer guide to nursing homes is *Nursing Homes: Getting Good Care There,* written by Sarah Green Burger and others on behalf of the **National Citizens' Coalition for Nursing Home Reform**. It offers step-by-step guidance on how to make sure residents receive good care and have a decent quality of life once they enter a nursing home. To order, write or call the Coalition at 1424 Sixteenth Street, NW, Suite 202, Washington, DC 20036, (202) 332-2275.

- **AARP** and the **American Association of Homes and Services for the Aging (AAHSA)**, listed above, both provide a variety of useful materials on nursing homes for consumers.

- Nursing home ombudsmen frequently prepare guides to long-term-care options. Any nursing home or your local area agency on aging will be able to tell you how to contact the ombudsman program.

CHAPTER SIX

Rights of Persons with Disabilities

WE ALL AGE DIFFERENTLY. Although we're living longer and in better health than ever before, there is a higher likelihood of disability as we age. A third of us over sixty-five have a physical disability, as do half of us over eighty-five. A disability does not mean that you must give up the places, activities, and livelihood you have been used to. Three important federal laws—the **Rehabilitation Act of 1973,** the **Americans with Disabilities Act of 1990 (ADA),** and the **Fair Housing Amendments Act of 1988 (FHAA)**—protect people with disabilities from discrimination. In addition, these laws require employers and providers of services to make modifications to meet the needs of persons with disabilities.

The Rehabilitation Act, the ADA, and the FHAA protect people with impairments that substantially limit one or more **major life activities**—such as:

seeing	walking	learning
hearing	breathing	caring for yourself
speaking	performing manual tasks	working

You are covered if you suffer from disabling, chronic conditions such as paralysis, mental retardation, a substantial vision or hearing loss, severe arthritis, or respiratory difficulties. The laws also protect you if you merely have a record of such an impairment or you are *perceived* as having such an impairment—for example, a person with a history of mental illness.

These laws do not protect people who threaten the safety or health of others, or whose behavior would result in substantial damage to others' property. Nor do the laws protect current users of illegal drugs.

THE REHABILITATION ACT

Its key provision is **Section 504.** This prevents qualified individuals with handicaps from being discriminated against by programs or activities that either receive federal funds or are conducted by federal agencies.

Section 504 was designed to put individuals with disabilities on an equal footing with others in regard to these programs and activities.

What is covered? A program or activity means any operation of:

- departments or agencies of the federal government, or state or local governments, that receive federal funds, and the following, *if* they receive federal funding:
    - public schools, including colleges and universities;
    - businesses principally engaged in providing education, health care, housing, social services, parks and recreation;
    - other businesses.

Examples of covered operations are post offices, courthouses, city halls, hospitals, and nursing homes that receive Medicare or Medicaid payments, and senior centers that are supported by federal money.

Section 504 provided a model for the Americans with

Disabilities Act, which expands on it to include purely private businesses and state and local governments, even if they don't receive federal funding.

AMERICANS WITH DISABILITIES ACT

The ADA aims to provide equal opportunity for persons with disabilities in:

- employment;
- state and local government programs and services;
- places open to the public such as restaurants, theaters, stores, banks, or senior centers;
- transportation;
- telecommunications.

The act does not apply to "private clubs" or religious entities, except when they sponsor public events. Also excluded are employers with fewer than fifteen employees. The only major area not covered under the ADA is housing, but the ADA's sister act, the Fair Housing Amendments Act, imposes virtually identical requirements on housing. The odds are that your activity or location is covered.

EMPLOYMENT

If you're a **qualified person with a disability,** an employer cannot discriminate against you in anything related to employment. You are qualified if you are able to do the job, with or without **reasonable accommodations.**

What is a reasonable accommodation? A reasonable accommodation is a modification that makes it possible for you to do the job. An employer must provide reasonable accommodations unless they would cause an undue hardship. Some examples are:

- changing work schedules;
- modifying examination or training materials;
- making facilities accessible;
- restructuring a job;
- providing equipment or devices (such as text telephones for the deaf or special software for computers);
- providing qualified readers or interpreters.

ACCESS TO PROGRAMS, SERVICES, AND FACILITIES

The ADA promises individuals with disabilities equal opportunity when dealing with state and local government services, programs, and facilities—like schools, senior centers, or courts. It also provides for access to the services of private businesses and commercial facilities—such as law offices, banks, or grocery stores. The ADA calls for three major kinds of actions by these providers of services:

AGE VERSUS DISABILITY DISCRIMINATION

Age is not a disability under the ADA. If you are forty or older and have experienced employment discrimination because of your age, you may have a claim under the Age Discrimination in Employment Act discussed in chapter 1. If you are an older person with a disability, you may have claims under both the ADA and the ADEA. For either law, you should file a charge of discrimination with the Equal Employment Opportunity Commission (EEOC) when the problem involves an employer.

- Making **reasonable modifications** to policies, practices, and procedures
- Ensuring the opportunity for **effective communications**
- Making **physical facilities** accessible

What are reasonable modifications in policies, practices, and procedures? These are changes in rules or practices to avoid discrimination. For example, if a restaurant has a "no pets" rule, it must make an exception to allow a guide dog to accompany a customer who is blind. However, modifications that fundamentally change the nature of the service are not required. For example, a museum would not be required to allow blind persons to touch art objects if touching would damage the art.

What are effective communications under the ADA? The service provider must make sure its communications with individuals with disabilities are as effective as communications with others, and must make available appropriate **auxiliary aids** and services. For example, if you have a hearing impairment and are called for jury duty, the court must provide an interpreter or an assistive listening device if necessary for you to participate as a juror. Actions that would change the nature of the service or be an undue burden on the provider are not required.

EXAMPLES OF AUXILIARY AIDS AND SERVICES

Examples of auxiliary aids and services for persons who are deaf or hard of hearing include qualified interpreters, note takers, computer-aided transcription services, written materials, assistive listening systems, TDDs (text telephones for the deaf), and exchange of written notes. Examples of aids for individuals with vision impairment include qualified readers, taped texts, audio recordings, Braille or large print materials, and assistance in locating items.

Do providers have to remove all barriers from their buildings? New buildings must meet certain design standards of accessibility. In existing buildings, private businesses must remove architectural barriers and make modifications (such as installing wheelchair ramps, or widening narrow doorways, aisles, and rest room doors, or making drinking fountains and telephones accessible) if the barrier removal is **readily achievable**—that is, able to be carried out without much difficulty or expense. If a barrier cannot be readily removed, the services must be provided another way. Public providers such as courts or libraries must make sure their program as a whole is accessible—either by removing barriers or taking other actions. A court without an elevator, for example, must schedule a trial on the first floor if a person who cannot climb stairs is involved. Library staff must retrieve books from an upper floor if necessary.

HOW CAN I ENFORCE MY RIGHTS UNDER THE ADA?

1. First, talk to the business, service, or employer. Explain your needs and what the ADA requires. Maybe you can resolve the problem informally.
2. Try mediation. Check with your local court or bar association for referrals to a mediation program in your community.
3. File a complaint with the Department of Justice if the complaint concerns state or local government programs and services, or private businesses open to the public. You must file within 180 days of the time the discrimination by a government program or service occurred. There is no specific time limit for complaints against private business.
4. File a complaint with the Equal Employment Opportunity Commission (EEOC) if you think a potential or current employer is discriminating against you because of a disability. Again, you must file your complaint within 180 days of the discriminatory act (see chapter 1).

5. Finally, file a lawsuit. Contact an attorney familiar with employment law for advice and representation. If it is an employment matter, you must file a complaint with the EEOC before going to court.

HOUSING AND DISABILITY

Sometimes, landlords refuse to rent to older people, or evict them simply because they need assistance with certain activities. Some renters are protected by two federal laws—the Fair Housing Amendments Act of 1988 and the Rehabilitation Act of 1973.

Section 504 of the Rehabilitation Act applies to housing programs that receive federal funds, such as public housing or housing for the elderly or persons with disabilities. The Fair Housing Amendments Act prohibits discrimination against people with disabilities in almost all housing, both government-subsidized and private. But it does not apply to rental buildings with fewer than four units when the owner also lives in the building.

Examples of prohibited discrimination include:

- refusing to rent to a family that includes someone with a mental illness;
- requiring applicants for senior housing to provide a doctor's letter stating that they are in good health;
- denying a resident who uses a wheelchair or a walker access to a communal dining room; and
- evicting a tenant because he or she is receiving homemaking help or other services.

WHAT IS REQUIRED OF LANDLORDS?

The landlord must make **reasonable accommodations,** changes in rules or procedures that are reasonable and that give a tenant with a disability equal opportunity to use the residence. Examples include:

- changing the date rent is due to allow a tenant time to deposit a disability check;
- providing large-print notices for a tenant with vision impairment;
- waiving a no-guest rule for a tenant needing live-in help;
- waiving a no-pet rule for a tenant with a guide dog;
- allowing a tenant to bring in supportive services.

Accommodations for disabilities often can be worked out informally. There is a limit, though. The landlord is not required to provide additional services that would change the nature of the business. For example, a landlord might be required to allow a tenant to continue living in an apartment while receiving support services from the county; however, the landlord would not be required to provide those services.

Landlords must also make or permit **reasonable modifications** to existing buildings to give a tenant with disabilities equal access to the residence. Examples include:

- installing grab bars in the bathroom;
- replacing doorknobs with lever handles;
- widening doorways for wheelchair access;
- installing a ramp;
- replacing small floor numbers with larger numbers so tenants can read them more easily.

The major distinction between rights in private rental housing and federally funded housing arises in the area of reasonable modifications:

- The Fair Housing Amendments Act gives tenants of *private* rental housing the right to make reasonable modifications to apartments and common areas of the property, but these changes must be made *at tenants' own expense.* Common areas include hallways, or even the entrance to the building. If you make modifications, you may be required to restore the premises to the original condition when you move out.

- Tenants in housing that receives *federal* funding have additional protections. Section 504 requires landlords to bear the cost of reasonable modifications, whether they are inside the apartment or in common areas.

In one situation, a renter in private housing does not have to bear the expense of certain modifications to common areas. If you live in a building that has space open to the public, such as for a senior center or meal site, that space could fall under the requirements of the Americans with Disabilities Act. Under the ADA, the provider of the service is responsible for the cost of reasonable modifications.

For new construction, the obligations are much clearer. Builders must meet specific design standards that allow physical access by persons with disabilities. To find out what buildings are covered and what these standards are, contact the Department of Housing and Urban Development (HUD) Fair Housing Complaint Hotline at the number listed below.

Enforcing your housing rights. Section 504 is enforced by HUD. The Fair Housing Amendments Act can be enforced by HUD, by state or local human relations commissions and fair housing agencies, or by the courts. Call HUD's Fair

Housing Complaint Hotline at (800) 424-8590 (voice) or (800) 543-8294 (TDD) for more information.

DRIVING AND DISABILITY

Cars are such a vital part of American life that giving up driving can signal the beginning of dependence on others. Older drivers have more accidents *per mile driven* than middle-aged drivers. Moreover, they are at greater risk of dying from accidents. Many older drivers are perfectly capable, but key driving skills tend to decline with age. Vision, hearing, and mobility may be impaired. Reaction times may slow down.

Many older drivers recognize their declining skills and limit their driving accordingly—driving less at night, less on highways, and less on unfamiliar roads. However, some drivers, especially those with dementia, may not be aware of their limitations.

The right or privilege to hold a driver's license is based on state law. The laws are enforced by state motor vehicle departments. In determining whether a driver's license will be granted, revoked, or restricted, states try to balance the need for public safety with the driver's need for independence and mobility.

License renewals. All states require driver's license renewal after some period of time. In some states, license renewal procedures are different for older drivers. For example, drivers above a certain age may be required to take a vision test, or even a knowledge or road test. The renewal period may be shorter after a certain age. However, age itself should never be the reason for failure to renew.

When can they take my license away? Your driving skills may be reevaluated and your license revoked if:

- you fail to pass a license-renewal test;
- your accident rate shows you may be unsafe; or

- a police officer, physician, family member, or someone else reports you to the license agency as an unsafe driver.

In some cases, medical review boards may give or review the results of tests. Researchers are working on better ways for doctors, review boards, motor vehicle departments, and older drivers themselves to assess driving performance and decide when a license is no longer warranted.

Restricted licenses. States also provide for specific restrictions on the right to drive. The most common restriction requires you to wear glasses or contact lenses for vision loss. Some states are beginning to allow limited licenses for older drivers with a history of accidents or traffic violations, or who have failed their driving tests. A **restricted or graduated license** might allow you to drive during daylight hours, at restricted speeds, with special outside mirrors, within city limits, only on nonfreeway roads, or only upon taking yearly tests. These restrictions could mean that licensing is not such an all-or-nothing option. For example, you may no longer be able to drive safely in dense urban traffic or at high speeds, but may

OLDER DRIVER AWARENESS AND EDUCATION

Be aware of any declining driving skills and look for ways to compensate. Get regular eye examinations. Check with your doctor about the effects of any medication on driving ability. Adjust your driving habits to cope safely. For example, avoid unnecessary left turns and rush-hour traffic. Combine errands more efficiently, or have someone else act as copilot. Take a refresher course in driving techniques—such as the AARP program "55 Alive." Look for other ways of getting around in addition to driving. Many communities have special transportation resources for older persons. Check with your area agency on aging.

be very capable of getting to the grocery store or the post office on less traveled roads.

Fighting a license revocation. Each state has different procedures for reviewing license revocations. Your state may provide an opportunity for a hearing or other administrative review. A medical review board may be involved. You may have a right to review of the agency's decision by a court. Check with your state licensing agency to find out your rights.

WHERE TO GET MORE INFORMATION AND HELP

AMERICANS WITH DISABILITIES AND FAIR HOUSING ACTS

- **The Office of the ADA,** Civil Rights Division, U.S. Department of Justice, (800) 514-0301 (voice) or (800) 514-0383 (TDD). You can talk to an ADA specialist about questions, materials, and procedures. Lots of information is also available on the Department of Justice's ADA page on the World Wide Web at http://www.usdoj.gov/crt/ada.
- **The Equal Employment Opportunity Commission (EEOC)** offices are listed in the telephone directory under "United States Government." You may also find the location of the office nearest you by calling the EEOC at (800) 669-4000 (voice) or (800) 669-6820 (TDD). The EEOC home page on the World Wide Web is at http://www.eeoc.gov.
- Each state has a disability rights agency, called a **Protection and Advocacy Agency.** These agencies provide legal representation and advocacy on behalf of persons with disabilities. To find the agency in your state, call the National Association of Protection and Advocacy Systems, (202) 408-9514 (voice); (202) 408-9521 (TDD), or see their home page on the World Wide Web at http://www.protectionandadvocacy.com.

- **Independent living centers (ILCs)** are private nonprofit self-help organizations that help people with disabilities live independently in the community. There are more than 400 ILCs in the country. They can help you with a wide range of information, make referrals for services, and assist in finding accessible housing. To find the center nearest you, call the department of rehabilitation in your state. A state listing of independent living centers can be found on the Internet at http://www.designline.com/designline/centers.
- The **Job Accommodations Network** provides information on accommodations for workers with disabilities. Call (800) 526-7234 (voice and TDD).
- **ABLEDATA** is a computerized database, sponsored by the National Institute on Disability and Rehabilitation Research, U.S. Department of Education, that contains information on assistive technology and rehabilitation equipment. In it, you will find thousands of product listings that can help persons with disabilities. Call (800) 227-0216 or see their home page on the Internet at http://www.abledata.com.
- **The Center for Universal Design** is a national research, information, and technical assistance organization, located at North Carolina State University. It evaluates, develops, and promotes accessible and universal design in buildings and related products. Call (919) 515-3082 (voice and TDD) or see their information on the NCSU School of Design home page on the Internet at http://www2.ncsu.edu/ncsu/design.

DRIVING

- **The American Association of Retired Persons (AARP)** sponsors the "55 Alive/Mature Driving Program" aimed at improving the driving skills of older drivers and publishes a number of useful materials, including:

- *Older Driver Skill Assessment and Resource Guide*, with questions, ideas, tips, and self-tests to help older drivers assess their driving skills.
- *Graduated Driver Licensing: Creating Mobility Choices*, a twelve-page booklet defining graduated licensing and describing state licensing practices.
- *Older Drivers Fact Sheet*, by the AARP Public Policy Institute, a concise overview of the facts, background, and strategies for safe driving by older persons.

AARP is at 601 E Street, NW, Washington, DC 20049 and on the Internet at http://www.aarp.org. Or, if you're a member, you can call AARP at their toll-free number: (800) 424-3410.

- **The American Automobile Association Foundation for Traffic Safety** publishes two useful guides:
  - *Drivers 55 Plus: Test Your Own Performance*, a sixteen-page booklet with suggestions for identifying and resolving problems of older drivers.
  - *Concerned About an Older Driver? A Guide for Families and Friends*, tips for driving safely as long as possible.

The AAA Foundation for Traffic Safety is at 1440 New York Avenue, Suite 201, Washington, DC 20005, and on the World Wide Web at http://webfirst.com/aaa.

CHAPTER SEVEN

Grandparents' Rights

MANY GRANDPARENTS TODAY are family caregivers, sometimes by choice, sometimes by default. With these responsibilities come legal questions and problems. Consider a few actual examples.

- Due to their mother's drug and alcohol problems, six- and four-year-old grandchildren have been living with their grandparents for two years. The landlord has threatened eviction if another grandchild moves in.

- When their grandchild's mother left her spouse because of his mental problems, abuse, and drug use, the grandparents allowed the child and her mother to live with them. The mother "just left the child with us while she did her own thing. The father ended up sexually abusing the child when he got time with the child so child protective services and the guardian ad litem recommended that we have the child." The grandparents incurred $10,000 in attorneys' fees, $5,000 in counseling bills, and took out a second mortgage.

- Grandparents had lost contact with their nine-, eight-, and six-year-old grandchildren. They learned that the kids were in foster care due to drug abuse and neglect by their mother. The kids were separated in foster care, and then the mother was killed in an auto accident. The grandparents used the legal system to reunite all of the children, obtaining guardianship and incurring large legal bills.

- Two grandchildren have been living out of state with their father and his girlfriend since the children's mother died. Due to three years of neglect by the father, the grandmother has been seeking custody. The grandmother currently does not even have visitation with the children, and has been threatened with physical violence.

Custody and visitation are regulated by state law. Public benefit problems involve both federal and state programs, and in recent years there have generally been cutbacks in programs.

So exactly what are grandparents' rights, anyway? The legal rights and responsibilities of grandparents involve two different situations. The first relates to visitation between grandparents and grandchildren who are in the custody of their parents or others. The second relates to **kinship care,** when grandparents or other relatives become the primary caregivers for their grandchildren because the children's parents are unable or unwilling to care for them.

GRANDPARENT VISITATION

Grandparents denied access to their grandchildren have sought legal help in obtaining visitation. These problems reflect broad changes in American society. The divorce rate has skyrocketed, and post-divorce acrimony between parents may result in restricted contact between grandparents and grandchildren.

Traditionally, the common law denied grandparents visitation with a child over a parent's objections. Parents were deemed to have complete control, and courts refused to interfere except in extreme circumstances. But with the graying of America and a greater activism of grandparents, legislatures have defined the rights of grandparents and given them access to the courts to enforce these rights.

All states have enacted legislation enabling grandparents to petition for visitation rights with grandchildren. These statutes vary a great deal (see next section). Grandparent visitation rights also are being defined by the courts, as higher courts interpret state laws and constitutional claims.

Grandparent visitation disputes are painful and disruptive for the grandchildren, their parents, and their grandparents. Going to court may intensify the emotional issues and create problems for the grandchildren in particular.

If you are a grandparent having difficulty visiting your grandchildren, your state law (or the law of the state in which your grandchildren reside) may allow you to go to court and seek visitation. Before proceeding, you need to be aware of several things. Grandparent visitation rights are governed by state law. If you live in one state and your grandchildren in another, you will need to find out which court has jurisdiction. In addition, you must learn about the applicable law and important court cases interpreting the law. The laws do not make granting visitation automatic—they just give grandparents the right to ask for visitation. Finally, consider whether litigation is your best option. It is emotionally trying, costly, and time-consuming, and it may not yield acceptable results. Consider counseling and mediation as first steps.

WHAT STATE STATUTES COVER

State laws usually spell out who may petition the court for visitation privileges, under what circumstances, and what factors the court should consider in deciding whether to order visitation. Since state statutes are all different, this section will discuss general trends rather than specific provisions.

Who may petition. Many statutes permit grandparents to petition for visitation. The grandparent-grandchild bond is unique and precious, and grandparents are uniquely qualified to provide roots and a sense of identity to their grandchildren.

Other states have extended the right to petition for visitation to great-grandparents, aunts, uncles, and siblings, and even nonrelatives with whom the child has a close relationship. These are additional people who can lend stability and support to children.

When a grandparent (or other third party) may petition. Most state laws lay out the specific circumstances under which a grandparent may seek visitation. The most common circumstances are the death of a parent or divorce of the parents. Other specified situations may arise when a parent is incarcerated, when a child is born out of wedlock, or when the child has previously lived with the grandparent. A few statutes list no specific circumstances, leaving it to the discretion of the court.

The standard for deciding whether to order visitation. Most laws say that the court must decide whether visitation is in **the best interests of the child.** This language parallels that of most child custody and visitation laws. Unfortunately, these words are vague and do not provide much guidance. A few laws do list specific factors the court should consider, such as the prior relationship between the grandparents and the grandchildren, the mental and physical health of the parties, and the preference of the child if the child is old enough to express a preference.

Visitation after adoption. Many state statutes specify the effects of adoption on grandparent visitation. An adoption completely terminates the legal relationship between the child and the biological parents. But what happens to the relationship between the biological grandparents and the child? Most courts have said that the relationship with the biological grandparents is terminated as well. This interpretation makes sense when the child is adopted by strangers. But when a grandchild is adopted by a stepparent or close relative, many state laws provide that adoption does not automatically rule out grandparent visitation rights. This situation commonly occurs, for example, when one parent dies, the child's surviving parent remarries, and the stepparent adopts the child.

THE "INTACT FAMILY" SITUATION

Should grandparents be awarded visitation when the child is in an **intact family,** i.e., where the parents are still married and the parents and children reside in the same household? None of the state statutes specifically allow grandparents to seek visitation when the nuclear family is intact. Some state laws are general enough to allow grandparents to seek visitation when the child lives with both parents, but it is extremely rare for a court to grant visitation under those conditions. The decisions made by parents about what is in their children's best interest are generally not questioned by the court without evidence of parental abuse or neglect.

MEDIATION OF GRANDPARENT VISITATION DISPUTES

Consider mediation if you find yourself in the midst of a family dispute over visiting your grandchildren. Mediation emphasizes communication, privacy, and self-determination. The parties get a chance to explain their feelings and needs, and to listen to the other side. Since the parties fashion their own resolution, they can be creative, and they tend to stick with their agreement. Mediation can be quicker, cheaper, and less emotionally painful than litigation.

Consider mediation at an early stage of the dispute. The longer the dispute goes on, the more likely tensions will heighten and positions will harden. Moreover, mediating the dispute prior to a court hearing will save the parties, and especially the children who may be called to testify, the agonizing emotional experience of undergoing a trial involving sensitive private matters.

Mediation may be available in your community through

private mediators, community justice centers, or mediation programs affiliated with the courts that may be geared specifically toward family law matters. Judges refer many child custody and visitation disputes to mediation as an alternative to trial. In some court systems referring visitation cases to mediation is mandatory.

KINSHIP CARE

The number of "kinship care" households is skyrocketing. **Kinship care providers** are nonparent relatives who are the primary caregivers for children whose parents are unable to care for them. These caregivers of last resort are most often older relatives, particularly grandparents. Over three million children in the United States currently live with older relatives. In at least one million homes, a grandparent is the sole or primary caregiver. This situation is particularly prevalent in urban areas, but kinship caregiving is increasing in rural areas as well. These "skipped-generation" families face a host of law-related problems.

LEGAL RELATIONSHIP WITH THE CHILD

Many kinship caregiving arrangements are informal—parents and grandparents agree that the grandparents will care for the children for a time, or the parents leave the children with the grandparents and don't come back. If you are a grandparent caring for grandchildren, you should consider establishing a legal relationship with them. This will make it easier for you to register the child for school, obtain medical and dental treatment, apply for public benefits, get health insurance, and so on.

State laws spell out the legal authority a grandparent may obtain. In most cases, the grandparent must petition a state court. You must ask for **custody**, or possibly **guardianship** of the grandchildren. Adoption is another, more permanent option. If you are raising your grandchild and wish to apply for legal authority over the child, find out what your options are. Learn which court makes these decisions, and whether you can go through the process without a lawyer.

In some situations, the state may step in to protect a child from abuse or neglect by parents. When the state child welfare agency believes that a child is in danger, the agency may go to court to seek custody of the child and permission to remove the child from the home. Grandparents may play a role in these proceedings as well, possibly as the reporter of abuse, or as a witness, or as a potential custodian of the child. If the state removes a child from his parent, the state generally retains legal custody, and the relative may qualify as a foster parent, entitling the relative to foster care payments (see next section). Court actions involving abuse or neglect have different names in different states—**care and protection cases, dependency actions, children in need of services (CHINS) cases,** etc.

Many families prefer not to get involved in the court system. Court cases take money, time, and energy. Families may not want to change the child's legal relationship with parents, especially if the arrangement is temporary. Grandparents may temporarily care for grandchildren to avoid the state becoming the legal custodian. State intervention may result in parents losing decision-making authority or other rights. Adoption terminates parental rights permanently. Therefore, informal caregiving arrangements are sometimes more attractive.

If you have not obtained a court order giving you legal authority to care for your grandchild, you may have difficulty getting services from school systems, hospitals, welfare offices, and other agencies. It is often not clear whether a parent can authorize another as a stand-in. Some states have mechanisms to enable parents to authorize others. For example, the

District of Columbia and California have enacted **consent** legislation, under which the child's parents can authorize another adult to obtain medical treatment for children in their care. The parents need only sign a simple document, and health care providers must honor the authorization. California's law applies in some cases to school enrollment as well.

Some new laws address the tragic situation of parents who are terminally ill with AIDS or other conditions. Under **standby guardianship** laws, a parent may designate a guardian for children in advance, and the guardianship will take effect when the parent dies, becomes incapacitated, or feels no longer able to care for the child. New York, Florida, Illinois, California, and Maryland, among others, have passed standby guardianship laws.

FINANCIAL SUPPORT FOR KINSHIP CARE

If you are a grandparent raising grandchildren, you may qualify for federally supported welfare assistance, discussed below, but these benefits provide minimal cash assistance. The other source of federally supported direct payments is the foster care program under **Title IV-E of the Social Security Act.** Foster care payments are substantially higher than welfare benefits, but are difficult in two ways: the children must be placed in state custody, and potential foster parents who are relatives must meet state standards for foster care. Some standards, such as those requiring a set number of bedrooms, may be difficult for relatives to meet. Some states have waived certain requirements for kinship caregivers and have provided support services in addition to monthly financial payments, recognizing that it is important to keep children with family members.

Eligibility requirements for public programs are complex and often inconsistent, and obtaining benefits can be daunting. Here are some benefits for which you and/or your grandchildren may be eligible:

- **Temporary Assistance to Needy Families (TANF)** is the federal welfare block grant program that replaces the former Aid to Families with Dependent Children entitlement program. You and your grandchildren may qualify if you fall within certain income limits. States have a fair amount of flexibility in deciding how to apply new federal mandates that impose work requirements and time limits on benefits. Contact your local welfare department or area agency on aging to find out the rules in your state.
- **Medicaid.** Medicaid provides medical assistance to low-income people who are blind, disabled, or part of a family with dependent children. Grandchildren who qualify for TANF or Supplemental Security Income (SSI) are normally eligible. In addition, some children whose incomes are too high to qualify for TANF or SSI but have substantial medical needs may qualify. You do not necessarily need legal custody of your grandchildren to prove that you are caring for them. See chapter 4 for more on Medicaid.
- **Food stamps.** Food stamps provide a monthly credit to purchase food. Their value is based on the number of people in the household and the household income. You may apply for food stamps at the welfare office, but you should also be able to get an application at a Social Security office. Again, you don't need legal custody of the children to obtain food stamps.
- **Supplemental Security Income (SSI).** SSI provides low-income elderly, blind, or disabled individuals (including children) with financial assistance. SSI is a federal program, although states may supplement the benefit. Grandchildren can qualify if they are blind or disabled and meet the income and asset requirements. A grandparent may qualify if elderly, blind, or disabled. Grandparents may apply for SSI on behalf of their grandchildren. If a child qualifies, the grandparent can serve as the child's

representative payee, so that the check will be issued to the grandparent on behalf of the child. You cannot receive both TANF and SSI, but SSI benefits are generally higher.

- **Earned income tax credit (EIC).** The EIC is a special benefit for low- and moderate-income working people, including grandparents raising children. This tax credit program, administered by the Internal Revenue Service, provides a cash payment *even if you do not owe any taxes.* Earned income must be below a specified level. For example, for 1996 tax returns, grandparents with one grandchild could earn up to $25,078 and be eligible for the EIC (with two or more grandchildren, $28,495). These eligibility levels change yearly. The actual amount of the credit is a percentage of your earned income but can be as high as $2,152 for one child in 1996. To apply for the EIC, you must file an income tax return. You may receive it as a refund at the end of the year, or you may receive 60 percent of the benefit in regular installments as an addition to your paycheck if you are working. You will need to prove that your grandchild is a **qualifying child,** based on age, residency, and relationship. The child must be under nineteen, under twenty-four if a full-time student, or permanently and totally disabled. The child must have lived with you for at least six months. The child must be a biological or adopted child, a descendant (which includes grandchildren), a stepchild, or an eligible foster child. Again, you don't need legal custody.

HOUSING ISSUES

Grandparents living in rental housing may run into problems if they add grandchildren to their households. In some subsidized housing for the elderly, you may lose your eligibility when children move in. In other types of public or subsidized housing, you may become ineligible for your current rental unit because your family size has increased.

Even in private rental housing, your landlord may try to evict you.

If you are threatened with eviction, consult a lawyer. Laws may protect you from eviction because you have children in your household. The landlord may not be following proper eviction procedures, or a public housing authority may not be complying with regulations.

APPLYING FOR BENEFITS

Here are some practical tips for grandparents applying for public benefit programs.

- Be prepared to visit the public benefits office twice and be prepared for long waits.
- Bring documentation with you. You might need your grandchild's birth certificate; your son's or daughter's (the child's parent) birth certificate; Social Security numbers; proof of income for household members; proof of assets such as bank statements and deeds; documentation of household expenses such as rent receipts and utility bills; documentation of your role as caretaker relative, such as a power of attorney, signed statements, or court papers.
- File the application, even if you need to come back with more documentation. Generally, your benefits will be paid retroactive to the application date.
- Don't be discouraged by unfriendly, unhelpful caseworkers or the volume of red tape.
- Get legal help if you run into problems. Contact your local legal services office, law school clinic, or bar association for information about free or low-cost legal assistance.
- Help applying for the earned income credit may be available through AARP's Tax Aide Program or Grandparent Information Center (see below).

WHERE TO GET MORE INFORMATION AND HELP

- **The Grandparent Information Center** at the American Association of Retired Persons provides general information and publications. The center keeps a listing of support groups and other resources around the country and also publishes a pamphlet, *Survey of State Laws 1994: Grandparent Visitation Rights.* AARP is at 601 E Street, NW, Washington, DC 20049, and on the Internet at http://www.aarp.org. If you're a member, call their toll-free number: (800) 424-3410.
- **Caring Grandparents of America,** Suite 302, 400 Seventh Street, NW, Washington, DC 20004, and the **National Coalition of Grandparents,** 137 Larkin Street, Madison, WI 53705, (608) 238-8751, are two of many other support and advocacy groups addressing grandparent issues. A list of these groups and websites may be found on the **GrandsRuS** home page (Grandparents and Special Others Raising Children) on the Internet at http://www.eclypse.com/GrandsRuS/index.htm.
- *Grandparent Visitation Disputes: A Legal Resource Manual* (1989), published by **The Commission on Legal Problems of the Elderly,** American Bar Association, provides a useful overview of visitation legal issues, although state statutes have changed a great deal since 1989. Contact the ABA Commission at 740 Fifteenth Street, NW, Washington, DC, 20005-1009 or see the commission's information in the ABA's home page at http://www.abanet.org/elderly.
- Your state or local **agency on aging** can help identify services and supports for grandparents with a variety of needs. Look in your local government listings under "Aging" or call the **National Eldercare Locator** at (800) 677-1116 to find the agency on aging nearest you. You can also search the database of the National Eldercare Locator on-line through their website at http://www.ageinfo.org/elderloc.

CHAPTER EIGHT

Consumer Protection

UNFORTUNATELY, SURVEYS SHOW that older persons are often specially targeted by con men. They are not the only victims, but they tend to have the characteristics that con artists look for.

This chapter will describe only a few of the more common consumer situations in which you may find yourself subject to deceptive or high-pressure tactics. Another book in this series, the *ABA Guide to Consumer Law,* offers additional guidance.

TELEPHONE SOLICITATIONS AND CREDIT CARD SCAMS

Telephone solicitations all involve some risk. You might, for example, be charged for items or services you never bought or requested. If that happens, notify your credit card company immediately and do not pay the contested amount. If you receive merchandise you did not request, Federal Trade Commission rules and many state consumer laws permit you to treat the item as a gift and keep it.

The most basic rule of thumb is to avoid giving your credit card number to strangers over the phone, *unless* you initiate the call to a number you are sure is legitimate. Do not give your credit card number if it is requested to "verify" who you are for some other purpose, such as for receipt of a so-called prize, and don't give out your checking account number or authorize the seller to take the money from your bank account without your signature on a check.

A federal telemarketing sales rule now makes it more difficult for telemarketers to misrepresent who they are and what they are offering. It is now illegal to claim that a caller represents a charity or sweepstakes promotion that is really a front for a sales operation. Likewise, mislabeling fees as shipping or handling fees or taxes is prohibited.

Another practice targeted by the rule involves **recovery room** operations, in which companies provide assistance with repairing poor credit ratings or obtaining loans, or in recovering money lost by the consumer to illegal telemarketing operations. Some of these companies are actually the same companies that defraud unsuspecting consumers in the first place. The rule prohibits payment until *after* the service is performed.

The rule requires that all telemarketing calls be made only between the hours of 8:00 A.M. and 9:00 P.M. (your time) and begin with:

- identification of the caller;
- the nature of the goods being sold and total cost of goods offered;
- details on refund policies or a disclosure that all sales are final;
- if a "prize" is offered, a statement that the consumer does not have to purchase anything in order to win a "prize," the odds of winning prizes, and any restriction on getting prizes.

It's illegal for a telemarketer to call you if you've asked not to be called. If they call back, hang up and report them to your state's attorney general's office or the National Fraud Information Center (see section at the end of this chapter).

PRIZE SCHEMES

Be skeptical of all prize offers. Many have long strings attached.

- You may have to purchase something in order to get the "prize."
- You may be required to pay shipping and handling (typically at an inflated rate).
- The value of the prize ("estimated retail value") may be greatly overstated.
- You may be obligated to make future purchases under a subscription plan.
- You may be required to sign an acceptance that, in small print, authorizes a company to switch your long-distance phone service to another carrier.
- You may be required to attend a sales orientation for some product or property. This, of course, sets you up for further high-pressure sales tactics.
- You may have to call a 900 phone number (which you must pay for).
- You may be asked for your credit card number for verification or for paying shipping. Don't give your credit card number.

To spot these scams, look for envelopes dressed up to look like official notifications ("Award Claim Number 88-7906"), first class or express delivery, or with official-sounding names ("National Prize Center" or "Federal Audit Bureau"). Be wary if the company is out of state and carries only a P.O. box address. Look for small print tucked away in the glossy notification material. If it is hard to read or understand, they don't want you to understand it.

State consumer laws and the federal telemarketing sales rule address some of the prize scam practices. You can always say no to the phone caller, or throw the mail notification away. Or check out the company offering the prize by contacting your state's attorney general's office, the National Fraud Information Center, or your Better Business Bureau (see end of this chapter).

DOOR-TO-DOOR SALES

Retired people spend more time at home than people still in the workforce, and are more likely to encounter door-to-door sales. Protect yourself by not feeling pressured to let anyone you don't know into your home. Ask to see the person's credentials. Many localities require door-to-door sellers to have permits. Contact your local business permit office to verify the permit.

Second, never say yes on the spot. Ask for all the information in writing, including price, warranties, all conditions, additional fees, and financing. Tell the seller you will review the material and get back to him or her. If the seller is uncooperative, call a nearby friend, relative, or the police.

Third, thoroughly evaluate the offer if you are interested in it. Check out the company through the local Better Business Bureau or consumer affairs office. Compare prices with those of local merchants. Be sure you know what the price includes (for example, does it include delivery and installation?). Make sure that any agreement is in writing, includes the address (not just a P.O. box) of the seller, and is signed by both parties. Never sign a contract with spaces left blank. Never sign a contract you do not understand.

All door-to-door sellers should tell you clearly that you have a right to cancel any door-to-door contract within three business days after the contract is signed. This is called a

cooling-off period. Federal law requires that the seller provide you with a written notice of cancellation, including a cancellation form that need only be signed, dated, and mailed by you in order to cancel the contract. Send it by certified mail and keep a copy so you can verify your cancellation. If the seller does not give you written notice of your right to cancel, you can cancel at any time.

HOME IMPROVEMENT CONTRACTS

Beware of the following danger signs of home improvement scams:

- Workers cruise through the neighborhood knocking on doors. They explain that they are doing other work in the neighborhood or have leftover material from another job, so they can give you an extra-good price if you act now.
- The workers drive an unmarked truck or one with out-of-state tags.
- They demand cash payment for the work.
- They cannot provide any references.

Take your time and follow these tips:

1. Don't commit, sign a paper, or turn over money on the spot.
2. Call your local Better Business Bureau, office of consumer affairs, or state attorney general to find out if any problems have been reported about the contractor.
3. Make sure the contractor is insured and licensed in your county or city. You can usually find the phone number to verify this under "Licenses" or "Business" in your local government telephone listings.
4. Demand that the contracts include a detailed description of the work to be done, materials to be used, and date to be completed.

Avoid contracts that say "work per agreement" or similar nonspecific language. And if there is any "guarantee," make sure it is in writing. Better yet, have someone knowledgeable review the contract.

5. Get other estimates, or at least call a local contractor and ask if the proposed work and price are comparable to what the local contractor would offer. Don't believe that the offer is good "today only" because the contractor happens to be in your neighborhood.
6. Avoid financing arrangements that give the contractor a mortgage or security interest in your home as part of the financing arrangement. This creates a lien against your home and could even result in foreclosure.
7. Hold back a portion of payment until *all* the work is completed.

Finally, if you suspect a scam, call your local police or office of consumer affairs.

CHARITABLE GIVING

Most charitable solicitations are honest, but unfortunately Americans lose millions of dollars to fraudulent charities each year. Before you give, know what you are giving to. Here are seven more smart tips:

1. Look for an identification badge or other formal identification of the solicitor, the charity, and the fund-raising event.
2. Ask for background literature that explains the charity's purposes, how it accomplishes these purposes, and financing, including how much of your contribution actually goes to the cause and how much goes to fund-raising and administration.
3. Check with your state's attorney general's office to determine if the charity is registered and in good standing.

4. Don't judge a charity based on emotional appeals of the person contacting you or upon its impressive-sounding name or cause. Don't be pressured by guilt tactics.
5. Ask how much of your contribution is tax deductible. Political contributions are not deductible.
6. Always contribute by check made out to the charity. Cash contributions are too easy for someone to pocket.
7. If the charity sends you a gift, you don't have to pay for it.

INVESTMENT FRAUD

Investment scams are among the most serious consumer frauds because your life savings can be at stake. Perpetrators emphasize amazing benefits if you act quickly—of course, by giving them your money. You may think you can spot a phony scheme a mile away, but it isn't always that easy. Hustlers may work patiently to win your confidence over time with friendly conversation having nothing to do with investing and then call one day offering you "the deal of a lifetime."

Watch out for:

- Unsolicited phone calls from someone you do not know selling an "investment opportunity." Some of the more common pitches have involved penny stocks, or commodities such as oil and gas leases, coins, and precious metals.
- Promises of high or guaranteed profits. All investments have risk.
- Out-of-state companies with only a P.O. box address.
- Instructions to send money quickly. They may even offer to provide express delivery from your home or bank. Don't fall for it. Private delivery services may not be covered by U.S. mail fraud laws.
- Small "investment opportunities" or advice that proves successful.

These may be a setup for convincing you to invest a large amount the next time around.

One investment scheme involves calling several seniors and telling half that the price of gold or some other commodity is going to rise and telling the other half that it is going to drop. The salesperson carefully avoids pressuring the consumer to invest. Whichever way the price actually moves, the salesperson later calls those who received the "correct" prediction to boast about his accuracy. After building up a good track record with some number of the group, the scam artist announces that "now is the time to invest" and urges them to invest big money.

Some con artists have even represented themselves as fraud investigators seeking the consumer's cooperation in catching investment con artists. The consumer is persuaded to permit a transfer of funds in order to catch the criminals. But it is the quack officials who are the criminals in this instance.

The easiest way to protect yourself from these forms of fraud is to hang up the phone. But if you wish to investigate the opportunity, request all information in writing, such as prospectuses, brochures, and corporate reports. Most investments are securities or commodities. Companies and brokers that deal in securities or commodities must be registered with the Securities and Exchange Commission, or the Commodity Futures Trading Commission, and probably your state's commerce department or corporation commission. When securities are sold through telemarketing, the Federal Trade Commission is also involved. See "Where to Get More Information and Help" at the end of the chapter for information on how to contact these agencies. They can help you check out the background of any individual or company attempting to solicit your investment. Keep in mind that registration with any of these agencies does not guarantee honesty of a firm or individual. Nor does it mean that any person is recommended. The responsibility to investigate rests with you.

HEALTH QUACKERY

Unfortunately, Americans spend billions per year on products with no proven medical value that are promoted as modern cures for age-old problems. Older Americans are a prime target for health quackery that does little more than drain their wallets. This quackery can even cause harm by keeping you from seeking medical assistance.

Follow these seven smart tips:

1. Don't believe claims of a "secret cure" or "miracle drug" in television ads, flyers, the advertising pages of papers, or in "infomercials." Typically, these advertisements look like legitimate news stories. Ignore testimonials from unidentified users of the product.
2. Don't buy a product based on a seller's claim that Medicare will pay for it. Check first with your Medicare insurance carrier to confirm coverage. Some products that have been marketed this way in the past include seat-lift chairs, bed and wheelchair accessories, three-wheeled powered carts, and transcutaneous electrical nerve stimulators ("TENS") used as pain suppressants.
3. Check first with a medical doctor before buying any medical device or product.
4. Be especially wary of products that promise dramatic weight loss or restoration of youth and vigor. Arthritis "cures" and "miracle" hearing aid devices have been especially common.
5. If you are considering a hearing aid, have a prescription or recommendation from a physician or audiologist first. Don't be pressured into buying a particular hearing aid. Review the hearing aid contract before buying. It should be in plain language

and clearly spell out guarantees, servicing, and repair costs and procedures, and your right to cancel and to receive a refund.

6. Don't trust claims of official government endorsement or hints that the federal government is blocking use of a product that has cured thousands in other countries.
7. Check with voluntary health associations such as the American Cancer Society or the American Diabetes Association. They offer reliable information about legitimate health resources and treatment options.

If you have purchased a product of doubtful medical value, report your experience to your state's attorney general's office. Attorneys general have the authority to prosecute deceptive sales practices. The Federal Trade Commission has authority to prosecute the deceptive advertising of foods, nonprescription drugs, medical devices, and health care services. If the seller might bill Medicare, notify your Medicare carrier or call the Medicare hotline at (800) 638-6833. If substantial dollars are involved, seek legal counsel to get your money back.

LIVING TRUST SCAMS

Living trusts, also known as **inter vivos trusts,** may be an important part of an estate plan for some seniors (see chapter 9), but they are not a useful legal tool for everyone. In recent years, marketing living trusts has become a consumer scam. Official-sounding companies promote living trusts as a surefire way to save thousands of dollars in attorney fees, taxes, and probate costs, and to protect privacy and avoid court delays. These scams use misrepresentation, scare tactics, and high-pressure techniques to persuade elders to purchase prepackaged living trusts at inflated rates.

Be suspicious of operations using names easily confused with a legitimate organizations, such as the American Association for Senior Citizens or the American Association for Retired Citizens. The similarity of these names to American Association of Retired Persons (AARP) is no coincidence. These operations often rely on home visits by a salesman to make their sales pitch.

Watch out for the following tactics:

- **Fake affiliation.** Don't believe they have some connection to AARP or that their product is endorsed by AARP.

- **Cost traps.** Be wary of exaggerated cost estimates for writing and probating a will. A living trust might be less expensive, but it is by no means always so. Talk to a local attorney to find out the typical cost range for preparing a will and probating it. Learn how long it generally takes to probate a will in your state.

- **Exaggerated benefits.** Understand that a living trust does not necessarily guarantee that you will avoid probate proceedings. Nor do living trusts protect you from the claims of creditors, or protect your assets if you enter a nursing home, or enable you to avoid death taxes. Moreover, some companies charge more to do a living trust than what a local attorney would charge. Some companies avoid disclosing the necessary cost of transferring your property to the trust. A trust does little good if no property is transferred into it. Be suspicious of "maintenance" or other add-on fees.

- **Boilerplate products.** Sales representatives are typically nonattorneys. They may claim that an attorney prepares your documents, but this may mean only that an attorney drafted the boilerplate language used in the company's documents. Trust documents need to be tailored to *your* specific needs in compliance with your state's law. The attorney involved, if any, is likely to be employed by the company and not you, and may not even practice within your state. Thus, you will not be getting independent legal counsel. Don't decide to do a living trust until you have gotten advice from an independent attorney experienced in estate planning and licensed to practice law in your state. If a living trust is appropriate for you, an attorney representing you (and not some company) should draft the instrument.

- **Package deals.** The living trust sale may be part of a "membership" package that includes discounts on various products or services. Be wary of these kinds of deals, especially sold door-to-door by companies you are not personally familiar with. Contact your Better Business Bureau and state's attorney general's office to find out if there have been problems reported with the company.
- **Time limits.** Do not be pressured. If the deal is good "only today," then it is probably no good at all.

FUNERAL ARRANGEMENTS

Funeral planning occurs at a time of emotional upheaval. Time constraints add to the difficulty. Consequently, you may rely too heavily on the advice of funeral directors, sometimes to your detriment. The Federal Trade Commission Funeral Rule and laws in some states enable you to get the information you need to make intelligent decisions. You have the right to get information about the cost of individual items and services over the telephone. And when you inquire in person, the funeral home must give you a written price list of goods and services. For example, if you want to purchase a casket, the funeral provider will supply you with a list that describes all the available selections and their prices. You can purchase individual items or buy an entire package of goods and services.

When planning a funeral, don't fall into the trap of thinking that the money you spend is a measure of your love for the deceased. Your budget and values should guide you.

Comparison-shop using the general price lists available from funeral directors. And get help from others, such as a responsible family member, friend, or adviser, in the planning.

To avoid the stress and financial burden of funeral planning during mourning, many adults prefer to make funeral arrangements ahead of time through **prepaid funeral plans.** Prepaid options play a legitimate role, but they also have serious pitfalls.

There are two general types of prepaid plans:

- **Insurance-funded plans.** Under these, the consumer chooses caskets, funeral plots, or other goods or services and buys an increasing benefit life insurance policy from the funeral director or cemetery owner. The price of the goods and services are usually guaranteed. Upon death, the policy proceeds are paid to the funeral director or cemetery.
- **Preneed trusts.** Instead of purchasing an insurance policy, the consumer pays the funeral director or cemetery an amount for guaranteed goods or services to be provided at the time of death. The seller holds the money in a trust fund.

Preneed trusts are regulated in many states, yet problems still occur. The worst involve funeral trusts that have been squandered or gone bankrupt, leaving aggrieved consumers without any benefit. Other problems involve substantial penalties for cancellation, hidden expenses, lack of earnings on moneys placed into the trust, the problem of being locked into using only one funeral home or cemetery, and high-pressure sales tactics. State law may differ on how abuses are addressed. No matter where you live, follow these common-sense smart tips:

1. Obtain itemized cost information and compare costs among funeral directors or cemeteries.
2. Before signing a preneed plan or insurance contract, review it with an accountant, financial adviser, or attorney.

3. Don't rely on sales representatives, especially in door-to-door sales. Visit the funeral home or cemetery and obtain information directly from the source.
4. Check with your consumer protection office, Better Business Bureau, insurance commission, attorney general's office, or funeral board to determine whether any complaints have been filed against the business. If you suspect fraud or abuse, stop payment on your checks and consult an attorney, consumer protection office, or attorney general's office. The quicker you act, the more likely you will recover any moneys lost.

WHERE TO GET MORE INFORMATION AND HELP

- The **National Fraud Information Center**, sponsored by the National Consumers League in cooperation with federal agencies, maintains a toll-free Consumer Assistance Service, (800) 876-7060, to provide consumers with answers to questions about telephone or mail solicitation, information about how and where to report fraud, referral services, and help in filing complaints. Their home page on the Internet is http://www.fraud.org.
- **Local consumer protection offices** and **Better Business Bureaus** are good starting points and helpful sources of literature on consumer concerns. They're listed in your phone book.
- Every state has an office of the attorney general that enforces laws against most consumer scams described in this chapter. They rely on consumer complaints to identify fraudulent operations. So no matter how foolish you feel for "being taken," complain to that office. Many attorney general's offices also provide helpful consumer protection information. Look for your state attorney general's number under the state or local government listings of your phone book. You can also find a listing of state offices on the FTC web page listed below.

- The **Federal Trade Commission**, Sixth Street and Pennsylvania Avenue, NW, Washington, DC 20580, is responsible for enforcing federal regulations dealing with telemarketing, door-to-door sales, mail order operations, and funeral arrangements. They also publish a variety of consumer information. Contact the FTC Public Reference department at (202) 326-2222, or TDD at (202) 326-2502, or see the FTC's home page on the World Wide Web: http://www.ftc.gov.

- The **Securities and Exchange Commission**, 450 Fifth Street, NW, Washington, DC 20549, provides information and help regarding investment regulation and fraud. Investor complaints are received by their Office of Consumer Affairs, (202) 942-7040. Their Information Line is (202) 942-8088, and telecommunications for the deaf are available through (202) 942-7065. The SEC home page on the Internet is http://www.sec.gov.

- The **Commodity Futures Trading Commission** can provide information and publications through its Office of Public Affairs, Three Lafayette Center, 1155 Twenty-first Street, NW, Washington, DC 20581, (202) 418-5000. The CFTC's home page on the World Wide Web is http://www.cftc.gov/cftc.

- **U.S. Postal Service**. Call your local branch for the regional postal inspector's office responsible for investigating consumer complaints. The Postal Service's home page on the World Wide Web is http://www.usps.gov.

- For problems involving coverage by Medicare of questionable products or services, call your Medicare insurance carrier or the **Medicare information line** at (800) 638-6833. For information on disease-specific medical products or therapies, contact the local branch of the voluntary health association related to the disease or condition—for example, the American Heart Association, Arthritis Foundation, or similar group. Also check the Health Care Financing Administration's web page at http://www.hcfa.gov.

- The **National Consumers League** is a nonprofit membership organization providing a newsletter, publications, educational services, and advocacy for consumers. They are located at 1701 K Street, NW, Suite 1200, Washington, DC 20006, (202) 835-3323. Their home page on the Internet is http://www.natlconsumersleague.org.

- The **American Association of Retired Persons** has many consumer resources on homeowner scams, telemarketing fraud, and other consumer issues. Their publications on funeral goods and services include:

  - *Final Details: A Guide for Survivors When Death Occurs*
  - *Prepaying Your Funeral*
  - *Product Report: Funeral Goods and Services*

  AARP is at 601 E Street, NW, Washington, DC 20049, and on the World Wide Web at http://www.aarp.org.

- The **National Consumer Law Center** is a nonprofit organization representing the interests of low-income consumers. It publishes several guides for legal advocates and a semimonthly newsletter. NCLC is located at 18 Tremont Street, Boston, MA 02108, (617) 523-8010, and may be found on the Internet at http://www.consumerlaw.org.

CHAPTER NINE

The Right to Manage Your Own Affairs

As we grow older, we face the possibility that we may become unable to take care of our own financial affairs or make our own health care decisions. If that happens, are you confident that your affairs will be handled smoothly by the person you want and in the way you want?

Planning ahead ensures that you will maintain control over important decisions to the greatest extent possible. Planning requires you to think clearly about such questions as: Who would I trust to manage my property if I am too ill to do so? Who would I trust to make tough health care decisions for me? How and where would I want to live the end of my life if I were terminally ill or so impaired that I could no longer recognize my loved ones?

Several legal tools help ensure that the people you trust to call the shots will have the authority to do so, and that they will make decisions as close as possible to the way you would want. These legal planning tools are like life or health insurance. You would be happy never to have to use them, but they're essential to your financial and personal security. And, by using them, you will also lessen the anxiety of your family and friends, who otherwise would not know what you'd want done if you can no longer speak for yourself.

WHAT IS INCAPACITY?

These legal tools are most important when you lose **mental capacity** or **competency**. There is no universal legal test for such loss, and laws vary from state to state. However, some general principles are important.

First, incapacity is always measured in connection with specific tasks. The question is always "Incapacity to do what?" Different legal standards of capacity may apply to different tasks, such as capacity to do a will, to drive, or to make medical decisions. Second, just because you can no longer do mental or physical tasks does not mean that you are *legally* incapacitated. A finding of **legal incapacity** requires a guardianship or conservatorship hearing in court. In a typical court proceeding, most states use a two-part test to determine incapacity. First is proof of some type of disabling condition—for example, mental illness, mental retardation, and/or Alzheimer's disease. Second is a finding that the disability prevents you from performing activities essential to managing your personal needs or property. Most courts will also insist that all feasible alternatives to guardianship or conservatorship have been explored before appointing someone to manage your affairs.

Most planning for incapacity is aimed at *avoiding* the need for guardianship or other judicial intervention. The goal is to set up personalized, voluntary arrangements for managing your estate or personal affairs if you become incapacitated.

PLANNING FOR MANAGEMENT OF YOUR FINANCES

The primary legal tools for managing the financial affairs of an incapacitated person are:

- joint ownership (particularly joint bank accounts);
- durable power of attorney (DPA);
- trusts;
- representative payee arrangements (especially for Social Security benefits);
- money management services.

In addition, guardianship and conservatorship are a last resort. They're discussed after the section on legal tools for health care decisions, since they serve that function as well.

JOINT OWNERSHIP

You are familiar with joint ownership if you ever had a joint bank account or owned a house or other property jointly. This is perhaps the simplest and most common form of sharing ownership.

Joint tenancy "with right of survivorship" is the most typical form of joint ownership. The "right of survivorship" means that when one joint owner dies, the surviving joint owner (or owners) automatically receives full legal ownership of the property. Joint tenancy with right of survivorship is a common form of joint ownership for:

- homes;
- stocks and bonds;
- cars;
- bank accounts.

Bank accounts. The key feature of a typical joint bank account is that either party has the legal right to deposit or withdraw any or all funds. Usually, these accounts will be *joint with right of survivorship* (see above).

Don't confuse a joint checking account with an **agency account** or **convenience account**, under which the second party whose name is on the account is not an owner but rather your **agent** who has authority to make deposits or withdrawals on your behalf. These accounts are really just another form of power of attorney.

Joint ownership is a simple and very common form of ownership, and it's a convenient way to manage the income of an incapacitated person, when combined with direct deposit of the person's checks. Moreover, if there's a right of survivorship, joint property automatically passes to the surviving joint owner(s) on the death of the other joint owner. Thus, it is a simple, quick way to transfer money at death.

However, joint accounts have plenty of potential for trouble (see pages 200–201). Therefore, it is best not to rely on them as your primary planning strategy. Instead, use a durable power of attorney, and for your major bank accounts make use of an agency or convenience account.

DURABLE POWER OF ATTORNEY

A **power of attorney** is simply a written authorization for a person you name to act on your behalf for whatever purpose you spell out. Two terms are important:

- The person creating the power of attorney is called the **principal**.
- The person appointed by the principal is called the **agent** or **attorney-in-fact**. Don't confuse this with an attorney-at-law. The agent does not have to be a lawyer.

What does "durable" power of attorney mean? A power of attorney is **durable** only if it continues to operate and be legally valid even after the disability or incapacity of the principal. Historically, a power of attorney automatically terminated upon the incompetency of the principal. But, of course, this is precisely the opposite of what we want today. We most need the power of attorney when we become incompetent. Consequently, every state has passed legislation providing for powers of attorney that are **durable**, that continue to be valid even when the principal becomes incapacitated. In most states, the durable power of attorney (DPA) document must state that it continues to be valid even after incapacity. Otherwise, it may not be considered durable.

Another form of DPA, recognized in most states, is the **springing power of attorney**. A standard durable power of attorney is normally effective at the time it is signed. However, a springing power is a durable power that does not become operative *unless and until* the principal becomes incapacitated. If you don't need it, it just sits there dormant. If you need it, it springs to life.

A springing power has two potential problems:

- It requires careful drafting to identify who determines that you are incompetent and what criteria they shall use. Commonly, you direct your agent and attending physician to make a joint determination of incapacity.
- Third parties such as banks are sometimes less willing to recognize it because they may feel that they need additional verification that the power is now in effect. (More on this below.)

How much power does an agent have? A **general** DPA grants the agent very broad powers. However, a few state laws restrict what an agent can do, especially with respect to real estate transactions.

A **special** or **limited** power of attorney grants the agent only specific powers designated in the document. For example, a special power of attorney might state:

- "I authorize my agent to sell my property located at [such and such address]" or

- "I authorize my agent to endorse checks on my bank account Number 12345 at First National Bank."

It is important to be as specific as possible in describing the powers delegated in any kind of power of attorney. Courts tend to interpret powers of attorney quite narrowly, so it's best to clearly spell out powers to:

- make gifts;
- give loans or support to others;
- sign IRS forms and tax returns;
- open safe deposit boxes;
- fund a revocable trust;
- change beneficiaries under a pension or life insurance policy;
- compensate oneself as agent;
- make health care decisions (we will discuss this under "Health Care Advance Directives").

No matter what power you delegate, you do not forfeit any control while still mentally competent. You can still make or direct any decision you choose, and your agent cannot legally override you or act against your wishes. You can also revoke the power at any time (while still mentally capable).

How to choose your agent. In most states, you can name any person or institution you wish as your agent. This choice is the single most important decision you will make in doing a durable power of attorney. If you become incapacitated, your agent will have tremendous power over your property and affairs. If there is really no one whom you trust to act as your agent, then a DPA is not for you.

You can name multiple agents to exercise all the powers jointly (i.e., all must agree) or separately (i.e., any one may act alone). The disadvantage is that any disagreement among agents will cripple the usefulness of the DPA. Even in the most loving and well-intended families, disagreements happen, especially under the stress of family illness. An alternative to using multiple agents is to require approval by a second agent only for major transactions, such as the sale of your home or other real estate. This provides the safeguard of a second person's oversight in major transactions.

The most common method is to name *one* agent and to name a **successor agent** or agents in case the first agent can't or won't act for any reason.

Writing your DPA. Do not run out to your local stationery store to buy a standard power of attorney form. There is no such thing as a "standard" DPA. Each must be tailored to your individual situation. It is advisable, although not required, to use a lawyer to draft your DPA for property management. (See chapter 11 for suggestions on finding a lawyer.) A lawyer can make sure that your document meets your state's requirements and that the powers you give your agent are spelled out in language that will be legally effective.

Many states are enacting statutory **short-form powers of attorney** to simplify the process. The forms require you to check off or initial the powers you wish to give your agent or to strike through those powers that you do not wish to give. These short forms make doing a power of attorney much simpler, although they are by no means foolproof. It is still best to seek advice from a lawyer about the authority you want to give to your agent.

Signing a power of attorney is fairly simple, but you must comply exactly with your state's law. Timing is important, because you must be mentally competent to execute a power of attorney. Of course, your signature as principal is always required, and many states require the document to be witnessed and/or notarized. Even if notarizing is not required by state law, it is standard practice. It reinforces the authority and credibility of the document and it makes the document recordable. If the document is to be used for real estate transactions, you must normally sign and record it in the same manner as deeds to property. Finally, although the signature of your agent is not required on the document in most states, it's a good idea, since it helps verify the identity of the agent.

Using your DPA. After completing a DPA, either give your agent a signed original or store it in a safe place your agent knows about and can get to. Your agent will need to show the document to any third party he or she does business with. Third parties may want to keep a copy. Occasionally, a third party may insist on having an original, in which case you may want to sign more than one original. Another option is to have the local court clerk provide you with **certified copies** of the original. These will contain the seal of the court or its clerk and a certification as to their authenticity.

Your agent should always sign documents in a way that makes clear he or she is signing on your behalf, such as "Mary Doe, as agent for John Doe." If the agent merely signs "Mary Doe," she may unintentionally make herself personally financially responsible for your obligations, such as a hospital bill. But if she signs correctly, she creates no personal liability by signing. Instead, she obligates only the estate of John Doe. If she signs "John Doe by Mary Doe," she does not make clear the agency relationship between John and Mary. She should still add the words "as agent."

Terminating your DPA. This happens in four ways:

- Your death terminates all powers of attorney, either automatically or after the agent learns of it.
- The document itself can spell out a termination date or event (e.g., "This power shall terminate on June 30," or "This power shall terminate upon completion of the sale of my house").
- You can **revoke** a power of attorney at any time simply by noti-

fying the agent. Naturally, it is safer to do this in writing, and some states *require* that you notify the agent in writing when at all possible. Third parties with whom the agent transacted business should also be notified in writing of the revocation.

- If your agent is no longer available due to death, incapacity, or other reason, *and* there is no successor agent appointed, the power of attorney terminates. In some states, divorce will automatically terminate the former spouse's authority as agent.

Example of revocation: "I, John Doe, of [address] hereby revoke the power of attorney granted to Mary Doe on January 15, 1997." This should be signed, dated, and acknowledged by a notary public, especially if the power of attorney has been recorded. ***Important:*** The principal should destroy the old power of attorney document.

Also remember, if the power is *not* durable, it will terminate upon incompetency of the principal.

POTENTIAL PROBLEMS WITH DPAS

1. **Will anyone accept it?** Third parties may not necessarily recognize the power of attorney. Third parties are banks, businesses, or individuals with whom your agent transacts business on your behalf. A few states require third parties to accept a DPA made in accordance with state law, but that does not rule out the possibility of problems.

To reduce problems, avoid putting in conditions or unusual features that raise doubts about the agent's authority. This suggestion may weigh against using springing powers of multiple agents if they are not commonly used in your state. Fortunately, springing powers are becoming more and more common.

Banks, insurance companies, and brokers sometimes have their own power of attorney forms and insist that they be used. Check with the institutions you use and obtain their forms while you are still competent. If it is too late to do this, your lawyer may be able to convince these institutions to recognize the DPA.

Normally, a DPA is effective across state lines, but you may need to have separate DPAs in different states in which you have property.

Staleness becomes a potential problem if it has been a long time since you created the DPA. Even though there is normally no legal time limit on them, third parties are sometimes reluctant to accept one that was signed a number of years ago. Review your DPA and other legal documents every few years, update them, and reexecute them.

2. **Preventing misuse of the DPA.** An agent stands in a **fiduciary** relationship to the principal, and must live up to standards imposed by state law. However, there is no automatic oversight of the agent's actions by anyone. If you become incompetent or frail, no one may complain or take legal action against an agent abusing authority. Besides, agents are usually family members or friends with little understanding of what it means to serve as a fiduciary, and abuse often occurs through ignorance of fiduciary duties. For example, a son acting as agent may assume that it is perfectly okay to combine the bank accounts of the principal (his father) with his own, but fiduciary duty requires that such accounts be kept separate. Agents should be educated (informational material may be available from your attorney or local courts).

Another way to prevent abuse is to include in the DPA additional safeguards, such as:

- requiring the agent to provide an annual accounting to you or some other named person if you are incapacitated;
- requiring the cosignature of someone else you name if the transaction involves more than a specified amount of money;
- providing clear instructions or guidelines for your agent.

The best safeguard against abuse is to choose only those persons in whom you have the greatest amount of trust. If there is no person or institution you trust, don't use a DPA.

TRUSTS

A **trust** is a legal arrangement under which a person or institution, called the **trustee**, holds the title to property for the benefit of some person or persons called the **beneficiaries**. The one who creates the trust is called the **grantor** or **settlor**. Trusts are useful planning tools for incapacity, because they can be set up now and controlled by you while you are healthy, and later continue in operation under a successor trustee if you become unable to manage your affairs. Unlike durable powers of attorney, a trust may continue in operation after your death if,

SOME TRUST VARIATIONS

- An **inter vivos trust** is one set up and made operative during the grantor's lifetime. It is also referred to as a **living trust**.
- A **standby trust** is a particular type of inter vivos trust. It may be set up without putting any property in it or by just putting in a nominal sum. The grantor then signs a durable power of attorney that gives the agent authority to transfer funds to the trust if the grantor becomes incapacitated.
- Trusts may be **revocable** or **irrevocable**. You can change or terminate a revocable trust at any time while you're still competent. In planning for incapacity, you normally use a revocable trust. If you have substantial assets, tax considerations may be a factor in deciding whether to make the trust revocable or irrevocable.

for example, you have minor or disabled children who need someone to manage their finances.

Establishing a trust. There is no special language or form for establishing a trust. But trust language usually is complex, technical, and lengthy. The tax consequences of your trust should also be considered, as well as its effect on any future public benefits such as Medicaid. Trust drafting really ought to be done by an attorney who specializes in estate planning.

Advantages of a living trust. It can provide for managing funds in case you become incapacitated. Trusts are accepted in the business and financial community and seldom run into problems of acceptance, as powers of attorney sometimes do. They can also serve as a will substitute and be structured to continue past the death of the grantor, so they may have multiple uses in one's estate plan.

Disadvantages. The main one is cost, which includes the legal expense of creating the trust, the cost of transferring property to the trust, and management fees. When a bank or trust company serves as trustee, it typically charges a minimum fee and an annual percentage fee. And it may have little interest in managing your trust unless substantial assets are involved—as much as $400,000 or $500,000. A family member or other individual can be named trustee, but the paperwork, tax returns, and property management tasks can be complicated.

Trusts may also have a negative effect in your future eligibility for public benefits, such as using Medicaid to pay for nursing home care. Medicaid frowns on most trusts, and its trust rules are quite complicated. Good legal advice is essential.

One other disadvantage is that a trustee's authority is limited to the assets that have been transferred to the trust. In comparison, an agent's authority under a general durable power of attorney can extend to all the principal's assets. A common mistake in using trusts is not funding them adequately. Funding requires actual transfers of property to the trust. But even under the most fully funded trust, other property such as personal effects are likely to be outside the trust. Thus, other estate planning tools such as a will and power of attorney are still needed to complement the trust.

REPRESENTATIVE PAYEE

A **representative payee** is quite useful in managing a person's Social Security check. It is also available for Supplemental Security Income, civil service, railroad retirement, Veterans Administration, and some state pension checks.

A representative payee can be established for an incapacitated beneficiary without going to court. Someone must apply to the Social Security Administration to be named as representative payee—or "rep payee" for short. Then Social Security determines whether it is appropriate, based on evidence of the beneficiary's incapacity. Medical and other evidence will be required. Once a rep payee is appointed for a beneficiary, he or she has the authority (and a fiduciary duty) to manage the income for the benefit of the beneficiary. This authority does not extend to any other income or assets. Under Social Security Administration rules, the rep payee must also file annual reports.

Your agent under a DPA cannot automatically act as rep payee. The agent will still have to complete the application. It is helpful if your durable power of attorney expressly authorizes your agent to act as rep payee.

MONEY MANAGEMENT SERVICES

Money management services, also known as "daily money management" or "voluntary money management," help people who need assistance managing their financial affairs. These services may include check depositing, check writing, checkbook balancing, bill paying, Medicare and insurance claim preparation and filing, tax preparation and counseling, investment counseling, and public benefit applications and counseling.

This assistance may be provided by an individual or an organization, for-profit or not-for-profit. Services may be free, offered on a sliding fee scale according to income, or at a flat rate.

If you are considering a money management service, make sure it has a system of cash controls to prevent, or at least lessen, the risk of mismanaging your funds. It should also be bonded and insured. Check with your area agency on aging to find reputable money management services—don't just flip through the Yellow Pages.

These services require your consent. You must be able to request or accept help from them (although some money management services also serve as court-appointed guardians when needed). Money management services may be particularly useful if you have no one you trust to act as your agent or trustee.

HEALTH CARE DECISION-MAKING TOOLS

It is a scenario we all dread: you suffer a stroke that leaves you permanently unable to care for your physical needs and, although not unconscious, you are unable to communicate. A tube provides all your nutrition. Wires and monitors envelop your body like a cocoon. What would you want done about your health care needs in this situation? Whom would you rely on to carry out your wishes?

There are many other possible scenarios. They all point to the need to plan ahead if you want to keep some control over what happens to you. Here are some basic tips and tools.

A **health care advance directive** is the primary legal tool for making health care decisions when you cannot speak for yourself. "Health care advance directive" is the general term for any written statement you make while competent concerning your future health care wishes. Formal advance directives include the **living will** and the **health care power of attorney**. These legal tools evolved separately in the law, but today they are typically merged in a single, comprehensive advance directive. AARP, the ABA, and the AMA have collaborated on a sample comprehensive form. You can find it on page 220 of this book.

The starting point is realizing that merely completing an advance directive form will do you very little good if you skip the planning process. The process requires that you talk about your wishes and fears and options with your physician, family, and whomever you will rely on to speak for you when you cannot. Think of the conversation as a continuing process, because it usually needs to happen more than once. Your views change as you age. And they may change dramatically if you encounter serious illness. For example, your thinking about end-of-life options would probably be different if you were a healthy age thirty-five, compared with a chronically ill eighty-year-old. Completing an advance directive form should be the end product of the planning process, repeated at various turning points in our lives.

Every state recognizes some variation of advance directive. However, confusion persists over terminology and types of advance directives. To clear it up, let's compare the traditional living will and health care power of attorney with a comprehensive health care advance directive.

- A **living will** (or "medical directive" or "declaration" or "directive to physicians") is simply a written instruction spelling out any treatments you want or don't want if you are unable to speak for yourself and terminally ill or permanently unconscious. A living will says in effect, "Whoever is deciding, please follow these instructions." On its own, a living will is very limited—it usually applies only to end-of-life decisions, and standard instructions tend to be general. Unless you have a good crystal ball, it is impossible to anticipate every future medical scenario.

- A **health care power of attorney** (or health care "proxy," or "medical power of attorney") is a document that appoints someone of your choosing to be your authorized "agent" (or "attorney-in-fact" or "proxy"). You can give your agent as much or as little authority as you wish to make health care decisions. The decisions are not limited to just end-of-life decisions. Appointing an agent provides someone with authority to weigh all the medical facts and circumstances and interpret your wishes accordingly. A health care power of attorney is broader and more flexible than a living will.

- A comprehensive **health care advance directive** combines the living will and the health care power of attorney into one document. In addition, you may include any other directions, including organ donation or where and how you prefer to be cared for. Because it is more comprehensive and more flexible than the other tools, it is the preferred legal tool. Many states are enacting comprehensive advance directive statutes with simple suggested forms. However, there is one caution. Be sure your instructions are carefully drafted, because they can sometimes be read as limitations on your agent's authority when you really intend them to be only guidelines. In some locations, lawyers advise clients not to combine the two documents, because of this problem. Whether it truly is a problem depends more on local practice and custom than on what your state's statute says.

Why can't I just tell my doctor what I want? Telling your doctor and others what you want is essential. Effective planning requires this continuing conversation among doctor, patient, and loved ones. If you don't complete a written directive, conversations provide important evidence of your wishes to help guide decisions later on, especially if your doctor records your wishes in your medical record. In a few states, oral instructions, if properly recorded by the doctor, can have the same legal standing as a written advance directive. However, both legally and practically, it is far better to prepare a written advance directive, too. The written advance directive will carry more weight and is more likely to be followed, especially if it supports and affirms your continuing conversation.

Will doctors and hospitals recognize my advance directive? Most doctors and health care facilities want to respect your wishes. However, some may refuse to honor an advance directive, perhaps based on religious belief. If a facility has such a policy, it should inform you at the time of admission. Doctors generally do not have the same obligation to inform you ahead of time, so it is up to you to find out your doctor's views. If a health care provider refuses to honor your wishes expressed in an advance directive, the law in most states requires that the provider make reasonable efforts to transfer you to another provider who will comply.

Most hospitals, nursing homes, home health agencies, and HMOs routinely provide information on advance directives at the time of admission. They are required to do so under a federal law called the **Patient Self-Determination Act (PSDA)**.

The PSDA is essentially an information and education statute. It does not change your underlying legal rights under state law or tell the state what law it must have. It simply requires that most health care institutions (but not individual doctors) do the following:

1. Give you at the time of admission a written summary of:
    - your health care decision-making rights (each state has developed such a summary for hospitals, nursing homes, and home health agencies to use);

- the facility's policies with respect to recognizing advance directives.

2. Ask you if you have an advance directive, and document that fact in your medical record if you do. (It is up to you to make sure they get a copy of it.)
3. Educate their staff and community about advance directives.
4. Never discriminate against patients based on whether or not they have an advance directive. Thus, it is against the law for them to require either that you do or do not have an advance directive.

Can you *demand* treatment that a hospital or other facility does not consider medically appropriate? For example, can you demand surgery for a cancerous tumor that the physician determines is medically inoperable? In general, the answer is no. But the effectiveness or appropriateness of many treatments is not always so clear. So, by all means, state in your advance directive treatments that you definitely want.

Writing your advance directive. There are all kinds of advance directive forms out there—both official forms created by state law and unofficial forms created by state medical and bar associations, national organizations, and others. No form is perfect for everyone. Keep in mind that the form is to aid, and not take the place of, communication. The form is a tool for planning and not the final outcome of planning. Any form you use should be personalized to reflect your own values, after thoughtful discussion with providers, family, and advisers. And after the form is properly signed, discussion should not cease. Your views are likely to evolve over your lifetime.

Your instructions may cover any health care issue, such as:

- conditions or levels of functioning in which you would not want (or would want) life-sustaining treatment (e.g., stages such as permanent unconsciousness or severe dementia);
- types of life-sustaining treatment you may want or not want and under what conditions;

- the use of artificial nutrition and hydration;
- instructions about any other specific medical procedure that may be expected, in light of your personal and family medical history;
- organ donation wishes;
- preferences regarding pain control and comfort care;
- preferences regarding other aspects of end-of-life care, such as your place of care and environmental wishes.

Selecting an agent. In appointing an agent, you will need to consider who your agent and alternative agents will be, and the scope of the agents' authority. A broadly drafted advance directive usually gives an agent authority to:

- consent to or refuse any medical treatment or diagnostic procedure relating to your physical or mental health, including artificial nutrition and hydration;
- hire or discharge medical providers and authorize admission to medical and long-term-care facilities;
- consent to measures for comfort care and pain relief;
- have access to all medical records;
- take whatever measures are necessary to carry out your wishes, including granting releases or waivers to medical facilities and seeking judicial remedies if problems arise.

Remember, you can also limit the authority of your agent in any manner you wish.

The choice of agent is the most important part of this process. Your agent will have great power if you become incapacitated. There is normally no formal oversight of your agent's decisions. Therefore, follow these guidelines:

- Speak to the person beforehand and explain your intentions. Confirm his or her willingness to act and his or her understanding of your wishes. That means talking honestly and openly about death and dying.

- Know who can and cannot be a health care agent in your state. Each state has different rules. Most prohibit your doctor and other health care providers from being your agent, unless they are related to you.

- Seriously consider naming successor agents.

- Avoid naming coagents. It adds potential for disagreement and logistical complications. If you really want co-agents, have a plan for what happens when there is a split decision among them.

- If you trust no one to be your agent, don't name one. Instead, use only the living will. Or limit the authority of your agent, by giving the agent authority over some but not all treatment decisions, or by requiring concurrence between your agent and physician.

Formalities of signing an advance directive. All states have some requirements. Most require two witnesses to your signature. A few require notarization, or offer it as an alternative to witnessing.

Find out whether there are any witness restrictions in your state and strictly follow them. You will comply with the witnessing requirements in most states if you avoid using witnesses who are:

- related to you by blood or marriage;

- heirs or potential claimants to your estate;

- your physician or other medical provider;

- employed by a health care facility that is treating you; or

- responsible for your health care costs.

For individuals in nursing homes, some states also require a state nursing home ombudsman or a patient advocate or another designated individual to witness the signing.

Changing or terminating your advance directive. You can change or revoke your advance directive while you have the capacity to do so, and no one can make a health care decision over your objection. You can revoke your directive orally or in writing by just about any means, although it is preferable to do it in writing to your agent, physician, and anyone else who has a copy of your directive.

If you want to change your advance directive, it is best to execute a new one, since an amendment will require the same signature formalities of a new document anyway.

After signing the advance directive. Your work is not over when you sign an advance directive. Keep the original in a safe place where it is easily found. Give a copy to:

- your doctor, asking that it be made part of your medical record;
- your agent, making sure he or she knows where to find the original;
- any successor agent or family member who is likely to be involved in decisions;
- any health care facility you know will be treating you in the future;
- your lawyer, even if he or she did not prepare the document.

Consider keeping a wallet card containing a notice that an advance directive exists and information about how to contact your agent. State and national groups distribute such cards, but anyone can create a homemade version. In addition, a few national registries of advance directives offer to make your directive available to health care providers electronically.

Talk to your doctor and agent to make sure they

understand your directive and have an opportunity to ask you questions. The more they understand your wishes, the better they will be able to carry them out.

Review your advance directive—at least every five years and definitely after major life transitions or events (e.g., retirement, marriage/divorce, major illness, birth or death in family). Legally, the advance directive continues to be effective until and unless you revoke or amend it.

Crossing state lines: Is my advance directive still good? Providers normally try to follow your wishes, regardless of the form you use or where you executed it. Only if you spend significant amounts of time in more than one state do you seriously need to consider executing an advance directive for each state. In such cases, find out whether one document will meet the formal requirements of all the states. As a practical matter, you may want to name different agents anyway if one agent is not easily available in all locations. The agent should be physically close to the place of care.

FAMILY CONSENT (OR SURROGATE CONSENT)

Most people assume that a spouse or an adult child will automatically have the authority to make health care decisions for them. And doctors and health facilities rely on family consent every day. But historically the law has been silent on whether family members, even spouses, have a right to make non-emergency health care decisions for their loved ones. Informal family consent may work fine, as long as family members have some idea what you want *and* family and physician agree on the course of care. However, these are two big "ifs." If family members disagree with each other, or with the treating doctors, then family authority to make decisions may be called into question.

In the last few years, states have begun to enact laws specifically authorizing family or surrogate consent and laying down some ground rules, such as:

- **Order of priority.** Most family consent laws provide a priority in which family members are authorized to act—usually starting with your spouse, then adult children, and continuing another step or two according to the degree of kinship.
- **Scope of authority.** The surrogates may be permitted to make all health care decisions, or only limited decisions.
- **Handling of disagreements.** Some laws require the unanimous consent of all members in the same priority level—for example, all of one's adult children. Some require just one or a majority, or they simply do not say. Most set up a judicial procedure by which an interested party can challenge the authority of the presumed decision maker.
- **Lack of available family?** Most of these laws do not help when there is no traditional family available, although a growing number of states include "close friend" in the list of permissible surrogates, usually after family.

The moral is: *Don't rely only on family consent.* It is far better to spell out your wishes and appoint an agent through an advance directive. This will also help spare family members the agony of having to make painful decisions without any clue as to what you would really want.

GUARDIANSHIP OR CONSERVATORSHIP

This is the legal tool of last resort for decision making and management of your affairs.

Generally a **guardianship** involves the court appointment of someone to act as guardian to manage the property and/or personal affairs of an incapacitated person (commonly referred to as the **ward**). **Conservatorship** typically involves management of just the assets and not the person. However, definitions vary, and to simplify we'll just use "guardianship" here.

In addition, **limited guardianship** is recognized in most states. Under it, the court limits the guardian's authority and tailors it to the specific areas of incapacity of the ward. Limited guardianship offers a more finely tuned and less restrictive approach to guardianship, but some courts have been reluctant to use it.

If someone is appointed your guardian, but you already have an agent under a durable power of attorney or under a health care advance directive, the court will normally determine whether the agent's authority shall continue.

When is guardianship appropriate? People need a guardian:

- when they can no longer manage their affairs because of serious incapacity;
- no other voluntary arrangements for decision making and management have been set up ahead of time, or if they have been set up, they are not working well; and
- serious harm will come to the individual if no legally authorized decision maker is appointed.

Guardianship is a major intrusion into one's life and should be used only when there is a serious inability to make or understand the consequences of decisions. The criteria courts use to determine incapacity were described at the beginning of this chapter. A decision to seek guardianship should never be based on stereotypical notions of old age, senility, mental illness, or handicaps. A person has a right to make foolish or risky decisions. These decisions by themselves do not mean that the person lacks capacity. A competent person chooses to run risks. An incompetent person runs risks not by choice, but by happenstance.

Advantages. The primary advantage of a guardianship is that if it works as it should, it protects the incapacitated person and the person's property through judicial control and monitoring.

Disadvantages. It usually involves a tremendous encroachment upon your fundamental liberties. Your right to make your own decisions about yourself and your affairs is taken over by someone else. The legal status of a ward under a full guardianship is similar to that of a minor child.

Guardianship can be cumbersome, expensive, and inflexible. Normally, a guardianship must be instituted by a formal petition to the court with notice to all parties and the opportunity for a full hearing. The court may appoint an attorney or **guardian ad litem** whose job it is to represent the interests of the alleged incompetent in the proceeding. A "court visitor" or other professional may assess the alleged incompetent's condition. Guardianship proceedings may be emotionally trying and embarrassing to the incapacitated person and his or her family. Once a guardian is appointed, a bond may be necessary, and the guardian must file annual accountings of all transactions undertaken for the estate. Moreover, the discretion of the guardian is fairly restricted. Many transactions or decisions may require going back to court for approval, including a decision to consent to or refuse a major medical procedure.

Finally, the level of real protection may be inadequate. Often states fail to monitor how the guardian is handling financial and quality-of-life decisions affecting the ward.

CIVIL COMMITMENT

Under involuntary civil commitment, people with mental illness or other mental impairment may be compelled to receive care and treatment. Civil commitment most often is temporary, lasting from a few hours or days for emergency evaluation to many months for treatment. Most state laws set a period of time after which the need for commitment must be redetermined by a court.

The specific legal criteria for civil commitment differ from state to state. State law defines the types of mental conditions covered by the law, and generally requires a finding that the mental condition causes the person to be dangerous to others or to himself. Some states include alternative criteria, such a having a grave disability, or being unable to provide for one's basic human needs, or needing treatment essential to one's welfare.

Civil commitment is used less frequently than guardianship to meet the needs of older persons who can no longer care for themselves. The standards for civil commitment are drawn more narrowly, and the interventions are more time-limited and targeted to treating specific mental impairments.

ELDER ABUSE

Elder abuse occurs when somebody neglects or abuses older people. Abuse can be physical or mental. Definitions of elder abuse vary from state to state, but generally include:

- physical abuse, such as hitting or shoving;
- sexual abuse, including fondling, sexual intercourse, and forced intimate contact of almost any sort;
- verbal and psychological abuse, such as screaming at the older person, name calling, and threatening the person;
- neglect, such as withholding food, shelter, medical care, medication, and other necessities from the older person;
- abandonment, the desertion of an older person by anyone having care and custody of the person; and
- restraint, such as keeping the person locked up.

Also included in most states is financial exploitation. This can range from outright theft to misuse of the older person's money. Cashing an older person's Social Security check and not using the money for the person's care is one example. Many states also would consider the misuse of credit cards and funds held in joint bank accounts as financial exploitation.

Elder abuse does not strike any one race, social class, or economic level. Over 75 percent of abusers are family members. The causes are complex, but a major contributor is severe stress from any number of sources. In most cases, the preferred response is to determine the root causes and provide the services and supports needed to eliminate those causes and prevent future abuse. When the abuse is serious or not amenable

THE FINANCIALLY ABUSED

Q. My son is using my money to buy illegal drugs. He is also running up large charges on my credit cards. His name is on my credit card accounts and my bank accounts. Since he is a co-owner of my home, I am afraid he will mortgage it or possibly even sell it to get more money. What can I do?

A. Even if he has the legal right to reach your funds, you may protect yourself from this type of financial exploitation. Ask your bank to help you transfer funds to a new account without your son's name on it. Write all your credit card companies and ask them to remove your son's name from your accounts. Have them issue new credit cards to you in your name only.

Seek help for yourself and for your son from your local social or family service agency. Many of them have experience in dealing with family difficulties of this sort.

Finally, contact a lawyer to see what you must do to protect your home. A free legal services program for older or poor persons may be able to help you. Your local agency on aging can help you find those resources.

THE NEGLECTED NEIGHBOR

Q. My neighbor is very old and sick. She depends on her daughter for shopping, cooking, and cleaning. However, her daughter often leaves her without food and clean clothes. Is there anything I can do to help?

A. Yes, you may report this neglect to your local elder-abuse reporting agency. This may be your state or local agency on aging or human services department. You may even report abuse and neglect to the police.

You should not have to worry about being sued for making the report. Most states protect people who make such reports in good faith. You may also make an anonymous report.

to voluntary solutions, court intervention may be sought to provide protective services to the older person or to criminally prosecute the abuser.

Every state has specific elder-abuse laws. You can get details on laws and programs from your area or state agency on aging. Abuse can also occur in nursing homes, residential care, and other long-term-care settings (see chapter 4).

WHERE TO GET MORE INFORMATION AND HELP

ADVANCE DIRECTIVES

Most hospitals and agencies on aging have information on advance directives, as do many state bar associations and medical societies. **State-approved forms** and state-specific information are also available from these two organizations:

- **Choice in Dying**, 200 Varick Street, New York, NY 10014. Their toll-free number is (800) 989-WILL. They also provide a living will registry. Choice in Dying also provides a great deal of information on their World Wide Web home page at http://www.choices.org.

- **American Association of Retired Persons**, Legal Counsel for the Elderly, P.O. Box 96474, Washington, DC 20090-6474, (202) 434-2120. AARP's home page on the World Wide Web is http://www.aarp.com.

The general **advance directive form** included on page 227 of this book is a fairly simple model. (It is also available on the ABA website: http://www.abanet.org/elderly.) You may also find it helpful to consider forms that go into much greater detail about possible medical scenarios and treatment options. These are two good models:

- *The Medical Directive,* by Linda L. Emanuel, M.D., and Ezekiel J. Emanuel, M.D. This directive, originally published in the *Journal of the American Medical Association,* includes six illness scenarios. For each, you consider possible interventions and goals of medical care. It also includes a proxy designation. It is available from **Harvard Health Publications**, Dept. MD, 164 Longwood Avenue, Boston, MA 02115.

- *Your Life, Your Choices—Planning for Future Medical Decisions: How to Prepare a Personalized Living Will* (1997). This is an excellent, step-by-step workbook to guide you through the planning process. Available from Helene Starks, **VA Medical Center**, 1660 South Colombian Way (152), Seattle, WA 98108; telephone 206-764-2868, e-mail: tigiba@u.wash.edu.

ELDER ABUSE

- Every state has an adult protective services program responsible for investigating abuse, neglect, or exploitation and providing services for victims. Your state's program may have a toll-free hotline for reporting allegations of abuse. Programs are usually a part of your state's department on aging or state human services department, and most have local offices. Look in your local phone book or call the **National Eldercare Locator** at (800) 677-1116. You can also search the database of the National Eldercare Locator online through their website at http://www.ageinfo.org/elderloc.

- Your local police department. Always call 911 in an emergency.

- Your local domestic violence shelter. Ask the police, your local social services agency, or area agency on aging what's available. Or call the **National Domestic Violence Hotline**, (800) 799-SAFE (7233). The TDD number is (800) 787-3224. The hotline is able to assist non–English-speaking callers.

- The **National Center on Elder Abuse** has fact sheets of some use to consumers (although targeted to professionals) and a web page (the fact sheets are on it). Their address is 810 First Street, NE, Suite 500, Washington, DC 20002-4267. Their web page is at http://www.interinc.com/NCEA.

- The **U.S. Department of Justice Violence Against Women Office** has posted the addresses and phone numbers of national and regional domestic violence organizations and state domestic violence coalitions on the web. They can be found at:

  National organizations—http://www.usdoj.gov/vawo/national.htm

  Regional organizations—http://www.usdoj.gov/vawo/region.htm

  State coalitions—http://www.usdoj.gov/vawo/state.htm

- Two other useful World Wide Web sites are:

  The Family Violence Prevention Fund—http://www.fvpf.org. Or contact them at 383 Rhode Island Street, Suite 304, San Francisco, CA 94103-5133, (415) 252-8900. The Family Violence Prevention Fund is a national nonprofit organization that focuses on domestic violence education, prevention, and public policy reform.

  SafetyNet Domestic Violence Resource http://www.cybergrrl.com/dv.html.

CHAPTER TEN

Estate Planning and Probate

PLANNING YOUR ESTATE is about caring for your loved ones and making sure that your hard-earned property is distributed according to your wishes.

This chapter introduces the basics of **estate planning**—wills, trusts, and other ways of planning for your death. It is drawn from another book in this series, the *ABA Guide to Wills and Estates,* which more fully explains these options. The other key component of planning—planning for incapacity—is covered in chapter 9.

TEN THINGS ESTATE PLANNING CAN DO FOR YOU

1. **Provide for your immediate family.** Couples want to provide enough money for the surviving spouse, perhaps through life insurance. Couples with children want to assure their education and upbringing. If you have children or grandchildren under eighteen in your care, both you and your spouse should have wills nominating personal guardians for the kids, in case you both die before they grow up.
2. **Provide for disabled adult children, elderly parents, or other relatives.** Do you have family members whose lives might become more difficult without you? You can establish a special trust fund for family members who need support that you won't be there to provide.
3. **Get your property to beneficiaries quickly.** You want your beneficiaries to receive promptly the property you've left them. Options include avoiding or greatly easing **probate** (the court process for distributing assets left in a will) through insurance paid directly to beneficiaries,

joint tenancies, living trusts, or other means; using simplified or expedited probate; and taking advantage of laws in certain states that provide partial payments to beneficiaries while a will is in probate.

4. **Plan for incapacity.** During estate planning, you may also plan for possible mental or physical incapacity (see chapter 9).
5. **Minimize expenses.** Keeping down the cost of transferring property leaves more money for the beneficiaries. Good estate planning can reduce these expenses significantly.
6. **Choose executors/trustees for your estate.** Your **executor** will be responsible for carrying out the directions you express in your will. A **trustee** carries out the directions contained in a trust. Choosing a competent executor and trustee and giving them clear directions is essential.
7. **Ease the strain on your family.** You can take a burden from your grieving survivors by good planning, including planning now for your funeral arrangements.
8. **Help a favorite cause.** Your estate plan can support religious, educational, and other charitable causes, either during your lifetime or upon your death, and possibly save you money in taxes.
9. **Reduce taxes on your estate.** A good estate plan can give the maximum allowed by law to your beneficiaries and the minimum to the government. This becomes especially important as your estate approaches $600,000, at which the estate is subject to federal taxes in 1997. (It will be raised gradually to $1 million in 2006.)
10. **Make sure your business goes on smoothly.** You can provide for an orderly succession and continuation of your business through estate planning.

DYING WITHOUT A WILL

If you die **intestate** (without a will), your property still must be distributed. By not leaving a valid will or trust, or transferring your property in some other way (such as through insurance, pension benefits, or joint ownership), you've in effect left it to state law to write your will for you. The state will make certain assumptions about where you'd like your money to go—assumptions with which you may not agree.

Depending on your state, intestacy laws may give all to a surviving spouse or may split the estate between spouse and children. If you are not survived by a spouse or children, intestate laws generally require distribution to your closest kin as defined by statute. Only by planning your estate do you exercise control over who benefits from your estate and how much they benefit. Planning also gives you the opportunity to exclude anyone you wish from receiving a part of your bounty, except that state law gives your surviving spouse the right to a share of your estate. This share varies by state, but one-third is common.

ESTATE PLANNING TOOLS OTHER THAN WILLS

A will doesn't cover everything. In community property states—Arizona, California, Idaho, Louisiana, Nevada, New Mexico, Texas, Washington, and Wisconsin—most property acquired during the marriage by either spouse is held equally by husband and wife as community property. (The major exception is property acquired by inheritance or gift.) When one spouse dies, only his or her half of the community property passes by will or intestacy; the other half continues to belong to the surviving spouse.

HOW MANY AMERICANS HAVE WILLS?

Percentage of adults age 55 and older with wills	70%
Percentage of adults under age 45 with wills	23%
Percentage of all adults with wills	40%

Source: American Bar Foundation, *1989 Survey of the Public's Use of Legal Services.*

Other property not controlled by a will includes trust property, insurance policies, individual retirement accounts (IRAs), income savings plans, savings bonds, retirement plans, and property held in joint tenancy with right of survivorship. Some states have a special form of joint tenancy for married couples called **tenancy by the entireties.** A good estate plan must coordinate all of these assets with your will or trust. Using them well can give your beneficiaries money much more efficiently than a will alone can.

RETIREMENT BENEFITS AND ANNUITIES

Typically, an employee retirement plan will pay benefits to beneficiaries if you die before reaching retirement age. After retirement, you can usually pick an option that will continue payments to a beneficiary after your death. In most cases, the law requires that some portion of these retirement benefits be paid to your spouse. Retirement benefits don't go through probate.

IRAs (individual retirement accounts) provide a ready means of cash when one spouse dies. If your spouse is named as the beneficiary, the proceeds will immediately become his or her property when you die. They also pass without having to go through probate.

LIFE INSURANCE

Life insurance is often a good estate planning tool because you pay relatively little up front and your beneficiaries get much more when you die. When you name beneficiaries other than your estate, the money passes to them directly without going through probate.

Younger families find life insurance important as a way to replace a deceased spouse's lost income, pay for children's education, and pay off major living expenses such as mortgages. Older adults are more likely to need only a modest amount of life insurance to cover the costs of death, such as funeral, burial, and hospital bills.

Planning questions include the designation of beneficiaries (i.e., proceeds may be paid directly to one or more named persons, to your probate estate, or to a trust) and ownership of the policy (i.e., the policy may be owned by you or someone else, even though the proceeds are paid only on your death). The answers to these questions have significant practical and tax consequences.

LIFE ESTATES

If you sell your home to a buyer but keep the right to live there during your lifetime, you have retained a **life estate,** and you have sold a **remainder interest** to the buyer. Life estates, along with other strategies for giving away or selling an interest in real estate while retaining a right to live there (e.g., sale-lease-backs, charitable remainder trusts), are discussed briefly in chapter 5.

JOINT OWNERSHIP

The most common form of joint ownership is **joint tenancy with right of survivorship.** It can be a useful way to transfer property at death, but it also has drawbacks. Family automobiles, bank accounts, and homes often pass this way. Older people often place bank accounts or stocks in joint tenancy with their spouse, with one or more children, or with friends. When one of the co-owners dies, the other joint tenant owns all of the account regardless of what either of you says in your will. And many states give the surviving owner instant access to the account. The transfer avoids probate, although it does not avoid estate taxes if the estate is large enough to incur taxes.

Should you put property in joint tenancy as part of your estate plan? The answer depends on your circumstances, but most estate planners urge caution. Here are seven smart tips about when to *avoid* joint tenancy:

1. **When you don't want to lose control.** Giving someone co-ownership gives him or her co-control. If you make your son co-owner of the house, you can't sell or mortgage it unless he agrees. If you do sell it, he may be entitled to part of the proceeds.
2. **When the co-owner's creditors might come after the money.** They may be able to place a lien on all or part of the house or bank account.
3. **When you can't be sure of your co-owner.** Your co-owner could take all of the money out of a jointly held bank account. (Some states have **convenience accounts** that avoid some of these problems while allowing the co-owner to write checks and so on.)
4. **When you're using co-ownership to substitute for a will.** Joint tenancy doesn't help if all the joint tenants die at the same time. Each tenant needs a will. Nor does it help if a younger joint tenant, your intended beneficiary, dies first. If you wish to give to several children, but name only one child as joint tenant, be aware that the one child may be able to do with the property as he or she pleases. On top of all this, joint tenancy can result in adverse gift, income, and estate tax consequences for either or both owners. It may also affect your eligibility for Medicaid.
5. **When it might cause confusion after your death.** Were bank accounts put in joint ownership with your child meant to help bill-paying or were they a gift? Convenience accounts can help avoid this problem.
6. **When it won't speed transfer of assets upon death.** Some states automatically freeze jointly owned accounts upon the death of a co-owner until the tax collector can examine them.
7. **When one of the co-owners becomes incompetent.** If one of the co-owners loses the capacity to make decisions, it may become

impossible to transfer titled property (e.g., a home, a car, or securities) without a court-appointed guardian for him or her. This is costly and cumbersome.

Don't confuse joint tenancies with **tenancies in common.** In joint tenancy, you and your co-owner both own the *whole* house. In tenancy in common, you each own a *half share* of the house and either of you may sell your half share without the other's consent (though not many buyers are interested in purchasing half a house). Another difference is that the share of each tenant in common passes as provided in that tenant's will (or trust), rather than automatically passing to the other co-owner as in joint tenancies.

INTER VIVOS GIFTS

Federal tax laws now encourage people to transfer property through means other than their wills, often before they die. Trusts are the most common means, but you can also make cash gifts.

Gifts made while you're alive (**inter vivos gifts**) are a good idea if you have a large estate. They can help you make an estate smaller and thus avoid full-fledged probate and lessen taxes.

You can give any amount to your spouse without tax consequences, but inter vivos gifts to other people beyond a certain size are subject to gift taxes. Current law permits you to give tax-free up to $10,000 per person per year ($20,000 if a couple makes the gift). You can make gifts to any number of people and they don't have to be related to you. If the gifts are made to a charity, you may also benefit from an income tax deduction.

Make clear whether a gift to a beneficiary of your estate is intended to be an **advancement.** For example, if you gave your son $10,000 to pay for a year of college the month before you died and in your will you left him $25,000 without specifying that the college money wasn't an advancement against it, the probate court might subtract the $10,000 and give him only $15,000 under the will. Your intention in making the gift should be put in writing.

Finally, gift giving can have serious consequences on one's entitlement to public benefits such as Medicaid (see chapter 4).

TRUSTS

Trusts can help you plan for incapacity (chapter 9) and meet Medicaid eligibility requirements (chapter 4). Trusts can serve many other functions. They can help you plan for the care of young or disabled children or grandchildren in the event of your death. If you wish to maintain some control over gifts to others, they can establish almost any management rules you wish. If your estate is large enough to require tax planning, trusts can play a key role in reducing your taxable estate.

A trust is a legal relationship in which a **trustee** (which can be one person or a qualified trust company) holds property for the benefit of another (the **beneficiary**). The property can be any kind of real or personal property—money, real estate, stocks, bonds, collections, business interests, personal possessions, and other tangible assets. A trust is often established by one person for the benefit of another. In those cases, it involves at least three people:

- a **grantor** (the person who creates the trust, also known as the **settlor** or **donor**);
- a **trustee** (who holds and manages the property for the benefit of the grantor and others); and
- one or more **beneficiaries** (who are entitled to the benefits).

The grantor of a trust can also be its trustee and a beneficiary (as in a "living" trust). You normally name a successor trustee to transfer the property to other beneficiaries upon your death or to take care of you if you were incapacitated.

Trusts can either be **revocable** (changeable) or **irrevocable** (unchangeable). Obviously, the former is more flexible, but the latter may have tax advantages.

Putting property in trust transfers it from your personal ownership to the trustee who holds the property for your beneficiaries. The trustee has **legal title** to the trust property. For most purposes, the law looks at these assets as if they were now owned by the trustee. But trustees are not the full owners of the property. They have a legal duty to use the property as provided in the trust agreement and permitted by law. The beneficiaries retain what is known as **equitable title,** the right to benefit from the property as specified in the trust.

If you set up the trust by your will to take effect at your death—a **testamentary trust**—you retain ownership of the property during your lifetime and on your death it passes to the trustee to be distributed to your beneficiaries as you designate.

There is no such thing as a standard trust. You can include any provision you want, as long as it doesn't conflict with state law or public policy. The provisions of a written trust instrument govern how the trustee holds and manages the property. That varies greatly depending on why you set up the trust in the first place.

Despite the flexibility of trusts, the truth is most older persons do not need them. They do have advantages, such as sometimes avoiding the expense and delay of probate and maintaining privacy. But their cost may outweigh their benefits. Your particular situation should be evaluated by a lawyer in your own state who specializes in estate planning.

WILLS

A **will** is a revocable document that provides for transfer of your property at death. It usually designates someone as executor to carry out its terms. As with trusts, there is no standard will. All wills are different. What you put in yours depends on what property you have, to whom you want it to go, the dynamics of your family, and so on.

Although the rules for making a valid will vary from state to state, the following guidelines generally apply:

1. You must be of legal age to make a will (eighteen years old in most states).
2. You must be of sound mind and memory, which means that you should know you're executing a will, know the general nature and extent of your property, and know the objects of your bounty—that is, your spouse, descendants, and other relatives who would ordinarily be expected to share in your estate. The law presumes that a **testator** (the person making a will) is of sound mind and memory, and the standard for proving otherwise is very high—much more than mere absentmindedness or forgetfulness.
3. The document must indicate that you really intend it to be your will—that you intend it to be your final word on what happens to your property.
4. The will must be voluntarily signed by you as the testator unless illness or accident or illiteracy prevents it, in which case you can direct someone else to sign for you. (Don't do this without a thorough understanding of your state's law.)
5. Though some states do allow oral wills and informal, unwitnessed wills in limited circumstances, wills usually must be written and witnessed. All states have standards for **formal wills.** In almost all states, the signing of a formal will must be witnessed by at least two adults who understand what they are witnessing and are competent to testify in court. In most states, the witnesses have to be **disinterested** (i.e., not getting anything under your will).
6. A formal will must be properly **executed,** which means that it must contain a statement at the end attesting:

- it is your will;
- the date and place of signing;
- the fact that you signed it in the presence of the witnesses; and
- the fact that the witnesses then also signed it in your presence and watched each other sign.

Most states allow so-called **self-proving affidavits,** which eliminate the necessity of having the witnesses testify after your death that they witnessed the signing. The affidavit is proof enough. In other states, if the witnesses have since died or are unavailable, the court may have to get someone else to verify the legitimacy of their signatures.

KINDS OF WILLS

Here's a brief glossary of terms used in the law for various kinds of wills.

- **Simple will.** Provides for the outright distribution of assets for an uncomplicated estate.
- **Testamentary trust will.** Sets up one or more trusts to which some of your assets will be transferred after you die.
- **Pourover will.** Transfers (pours over) some or all of your assets to a trust that you had already established before you signed the will.
- **Joint will.** One document, which might constitute a contract, that covers both a husband and wife (or any two people). Joint wills often result in litigation.
- **Living will.** Not really a will at all, since it has force while you are still alive and doesn't dispose of property. Instead, it tells doctors and hospitals your end-of-life treatment wishes (see chapter 9).

If your will doesn't meet these conditions, it might be disallowed by a court and your estate would then be distributed according to any previous will or under your state's intestacy laws.

Legally, you don't have to use a lawyer to write your will. If it meets the legal requirements in your state, a will is valid whether you wrote it with a lawyer's help or not. Nonetheless, studies show that more than 85 percent of Americans who have wills used a lawyer's help in preparing them. It is especially advisable to use a lawyer if you own a business, or if your estate is substantial (a $600,000 estate makes tax planning a factor under current federal law), or if you anticipate a challenge to the will from a disgruntled relative or anyone else.

PROBATE

Probate is the process by which assets are gathered, applied to pay debts, taxes, and expenses of administration, and then distributed to beneficiaries of the will, all under court oversight. Many people think that probate should be shunned if at all possible. But times have changed, and probate is seldom the expensive, time-consuming beast it once was. Avoiding probate may be a primary goal of some estate plans, but for many others, it can actually be more trouble and expense to avoid probate than to go through it.

Three kinds of probate administration could apply to your situation:

- **Supervised administration.** This is the most formal and expensive method. The court plays an active role in approving each transaction. In states where it's optional, supervised administration is used when an estate is contested, when an interested party requests it, or when the executor's ability is questioned.
- **Unsupervised or independent administration.** This is a simpler, cheaper method in which the number of duties and procedures is

reduced and the court's role is diminished or eliminated. It's used for estates that exceed the asset limit for small estate administration (see below) but don't require heavy court supervision. It often requires consent of all beneficiaries, unless the will specifically requests unsupervised administration.

- **Small estate administration.** The simplest and fastest method of transferring property at death other than joint tenancy or payable on death accounts is through the use of a small estate affidavit for estates ranging from $1,000 to $100,000, depending on state law. This approach is particularly advantageous when the bulk of the estate is in a trust and only an automobile or small bank account is in the name of the decedent at the time of death. No court administration is required.

The details of probate vary by state. Discuss with a legal adviser whether avoiding probate should be one of your principal estate-planning goals.

WHERE TO GET MORE HELP AND INFORMATION

- *American Bar Association Guide to Wills and Estates: Everything You Need to Know About Wills, Trusts, Estates, and Taxes.* This is a separate paperback volume in the Times Books/ABA series of legal guides, available in bookstores or directly from the publisher at (800) 733-3000. It covers the subject of this chapter in much more detail. Other resources may be found on the ABA's home page on the World Wide Web at http://www.abanet.org.

- The **American Association of Retired Persons** provides a wide variety of consumer publications and other valuable information for senior consumers such as the following title: *Final Details: A Guide for Survivors When Death Occurs.* AARP is at 601 E Street,

NW, Washington, DC 20049, and on the World Wide Web at http://www.aarp.org.

- **Nolo Press** publishes numerous self-help guides on a variety of legal topics including estate planning. Nolo is at 950 Parker Street, Berkeley, CA 94710, and on the World Wide Web at http://www.nolo.com.

To find a lawyer qualified to prepare your estate plan, see chapter 11.

CHAPTER ELEVEN

Finding Help

PREVIOUS CHAPTERS in this book help you deal with questions you may encounter as a senior adult. Many can be handled by yourself, but some may require professional legal help. This chapter contains some guidelines.

DO I NEED A LAWYER?

With a basic knowledge of the law and how to use it, you can handle many of the tasks and challenges you face. However, major decisions occasionally need the help of a lawyer, especially if they involve complex facts or significant amounts of money, property, time, or personal freedom. Especially in estate planning, both financial and personal, be sure to seek competent legal advice. Choices made in this area fundamentally affect you and your family.

If you're not sure whether you need legal help, ask your clergy, or a counselor, social worker, financial adviser, or trusted friend to help you decide whether this issue needs legal assistance or social service help, medical advice, or some other form of problem resolution.

If a dispute is involved, determine if resources exist in your community to resolve problems informally, such as through mediation.

RESOLVING DISPUTES ON YOUR OWN

If you run into problems with consumer goods or services or a public agency, you may be able to resolve the dispute on your own. Self-advocacy requires good negotiating skills, which we all possess to varying degrees. If you decide to go it alone, keep in mind the following eight tips:

1. Always know the name and position of the person you are talking to.
2. Go up the chain of command. Ask the name, title, and means of contacting the person who has the authority to do what you are asking.
3. Bring a friend. Sometimes there is added support in numbers, and it is easier to record and remember information. But work out ahead of time the role each of you will play.
4. Get and keep copies of everything—letters, receipts, records, your own notes, and other documents. Make written notes of any contact.
5. Ask exactly what law, regulation, contract provision, or additional authority the other person is relying upon. Ask for a copy. Don't take the other person's interpretation for granted.
6. Find points of compromise. Try to clarify the primary issues and identify the areas where agreement can be reached.
7. Get any agreement or determination in writing! In disputes involving public benefits, you almost always have a right to a written determination, and a right to a formal appeal.
8. Remember the importance of ATTITUDE!
    - Treat the other person as a person. Focus on the issues, not personality.
    - Be honest.
    - Start with the assumption that the other person is interested in a fair and efficient resolution.

- Don't lose control. Controlled, genuine anger can be appropriate, but a blowup usually stops communication.

MEDIATION

Many disputes can be addressed through **mediation** or other means of dispute resolution. In mediation, a trained neutral person helps parties come to an acceptable agreement. Each side tells his or her story, and the mediator helps them think of ways the problem could be solved. If mediation does not work, you can still bring a legal action in court.

Many localities have court-based dispute resolution programs. Some have community dispute resolution centers or private mediation offices. Check the telephone book or ask the local court clerk's office, bar association, or consumer affairs office.

HOW DO I FIND THE RIGHT LAWYER?

Problems directly related to your age might be addressed by an elder-law attorney (see resources section at end of chapter), but many lawyers who do not call themselves elder-law specialists may be able to meet your needs. And older persons frequently face the same legal problems as other adults, and simply need to find a lawyer skilled in that area.

There is no "surefire" way to locate the best attorney. Many people rely on their own or a friend's contacts. Or you can do some research. Many local agencies and support groups have experience with high-quality local attorneys. Some of the agencies to contact include:

- the Alzheimer's Association;
- other specific disease support groups (e.g., Lung Association, Heart Association);

- your local area agency on aging;
- membership organizations such as the Older Women's League or the American Association of Retired Persons;
- state or local bar associations (they commonly operate lawyer-referral services available through local or 800 numbers).

At least twelve states (as of March 1997), plus the District of Columbia and Puerto Rico, operate toll-free statewide legal hotlines for senior citizens, and the number is growing. A listing of hotlines is included at the end of this chapter. Legal hotlines provide seniors with information and advice on simple matters directly over the phone; they refer callers to local attorneys if more extensive assistance is needed. Hotlines provide referrals to free or reduced-cost legal assistance for people who meet low-income guidelines.

Most communities offer some form of publicly funded legal assistance for older people, with attorneys, paralegal staff, and advocates who specialize in the rights of older persons. Your state or local agency on aging can refer you to these programs, or to a legal aid office offering more general help.

State and local bar associations may also have information about pro bono programs, which operate for the good of the public and do not charge lawyers' fees.

If you are homebound and want to speak to a lawyer, your local agency on aging might be able to provide help in finding a lawyer who can come to your home. If you live in a nursing home, you should speak with the nursing home ombudsman (see section on nursing home care in chapter 5).

National organizations may also help you find the right lawyer. The listing at the end of the chapter tells you how to contact them.

WHAT QUESTIONS SHOULD I ASK IN SELECTING A LAWYER?

No matter what specialization a lawyer has or advertises, it's best to verify for yourself whether he or she will be able to meet your needs. During your first call, ask the attorney or the attorney's secretary or office manager:

1. How long has the lawyer been in practice?
2. What percentage of the lawyer's practice is devoted to your type of legal problem?
3. If the lawyer specializes in the area of law you are seeking, how long has the attorney specialized? What specialty memberships or certifications does he or she have?
4. Is there a fee for the first consultation, and, if so, how much is it?
5. Can the lawyer provide you with references to clients he or she served with similar needs?
6. If an appointment is made: What information should you bring with you to the initial consultation?

Once you have an appointment, come prepared to summarize the facts of your situation briefly and accurately (providing a written summary really helps). After you have explained your situation, ask:

1. What will it take to handle the matter and how long? Are there alternative courses of action? What are the advantages and disadvantages of each?
2. What experience does the lawyer have in handling this particular type of matter? (This is the same as the initial inquiry, suggested above, but this time, it is based upon your particular circumstances, which the lawyer now knows in detail.)
3. If the matter involves a dispute, what are the outcomes the lawyer expects (including time involved, costs, size of awards, and burdens on you personally)?

4. Exactly who will be involved in working on your case and how? What experience and expertise do these others have?
5. What will it cost, and how will you be billed?

Finally, consider your "comfort level" with this attorney. This involves personal style or personality, physical environment, office organization and staffing, and convenience (e.g., convenient office hours, availability by phone, willingness to conduct home visits).

WHAT TYPE OF FEE AGREEMENT SHOULD I CONSIDER?

There is no standard fee or fee arrangement for most cases, so you should discuss fees openly and fully on your first meeting with an attorney. Some charge a **flat fee** for all or part of their services, especially if the service is relatively routine. If a flat fee is charged, ask whether incidental costs (such as photocopying, long-distance telephone calls, court filing fees, or delivery fees) are included. If not, get an estimate of these expenses.

Many attorneys charge an **hourly fee,** with different rates for different kinds of work (e.g., in-court versus out-of-court) or for work performed by different personnel (e.g., attorney, paralegal, or secretary). Again, incidental or out-of-pocket costs are often charged separately. Ask for a fair estimate of time and expense.

Contingency fees are common when money damages are sought, such as in personal injury cases. If you win, the attorney receives an agreed-upon percentage of the recovery, commonly one-third. If you lose, the attorney gets no fee, although you will still have to pay expenses, such as filing fees, deposition expenses, and other incidental costs.

The attorney may ask for a **retainer.** This is money paid up front and usually placed in a trust account. Each time the attorney bills you, he or she debits the trust account.

Find out the billing procedure and the amount of detail you can expect. In how much detail will the bills itemize work done, time spent, personnel involved, and nature of incidental expenses?

Make sure the arrangement is clear and reasonable. Get it in writing with sufficient detail so that you know exactly what to expect. Most lawyers use a written agreement, called a **retainer agreement** (even if no retainer fee is required up front). The agreement should be adapted to your specific situation.

WHAT HAPPENS AFTER I HIRE A LAWYER?

Good communication is the main factor determining how positive your experience will be. This starts by asking the kinds of questions contained in this chapter and continues with both lawyer and client keeping each other adequately informed and involved. The lawyer is ethically bound to defer to you as the decision maker in all major decisions regarding outcomes or objectives, and to keep you reasonably informed of progress. It is helpful to educate yourself about the general area of law or particular task the lawyer is handling for you. This will help you understand the decisions you must make and help you to assist your attorney more effectively.

If your lawyer's style or specific actions are unacceptable, discuss it immediately with him or her. If you cannot work it out, you may be better off ending the relationship. You still must pay for work actually completed, but doing this sooner rather than later will limit your costs and grief in the long run. If a problem arises that involves possible misconduct by your lawyer, and it cannot be informally resolved to your satisfaction, you may file a complaint with the state bar's disciplinary division.

WHERE TO GET MORE INFORMATION AND HELP

- *Finding Legal Help: An Older Person's Guide* is an excellent twenty-page guide produced by **Legal Counsel for the Elderly,** a program of the American Association of Retired Persons Foundation. Send $2 to Legal Counsel for the Elderly, P.O. Box 96474, Washington, DC 20090-6474. The home page of AARP on the World Wide Web is http://www.aarp.org.
- The **American Bar Association's Section of Real Property, Probate and Trust Law** offers a free directory of members who serve on its committees. This is one of the most active and productive sections within the ABA, and many of its members practice estate planning, estate and trust administration, and disability planning. The directory of members gives you the names of thousands of attorneys, and committee memberships help highlight their interests and expertise. Write the Section at American Bar Association, 750 North Lake Shore Drive, Mail Stop 7.1, Chicago, IL 60611, or call (312) 988-5590. You can also find out more information about the Section in the ABA's home page on the World Wide Web at http://www.abanet.org.
- The **National Academy of Elder Law Attorneys (NAELA)** publishes a directory of elder-law attorney members, including those certified in elder law by the National Elder Law Foundation. NAELA also provides consumer publications for older persons and their families. NAELA is at 1604 North Country Club, Tucson, AZ 85716, and on the World Wide Web at http://www.naela.com.
- **The National Elder Law Foundation (NELF)** certifies lawyers in the area of elder law by means of examination, experience, and

other requirements. This certification program, accredited by the ABA, has been in effect only since 1994. The specialty is still new and evolving, so many qualified lawyers have not sought certification. Contact the foundation through NAELA (above).

- The **American College of Trust and Estate Counsel (ACTEC)** offers a membership listing of lawyers by state whose practices concentrate in estate planning. To obtain a listing for your state, write to ACTEC at 3415 South Sepulveda Boulevard, Suite 330, Los Angeles, CA 90034. Their home page on the World Wide Web is http://www.actec.org.
- **National Association of Estate Planners and Councils** can provide a listing of attorneys certified in estate planning through experience, education, and examination. (However, be aware that many estate-planning specialists have not sought certification and so are not listed.) Call or write the association at 270 South Bryn Mawr Avenue, P.O. Box 46, Bryn Mawr, PA 19010-2196, (610) 526-1389.
- The **American Bar Association Section on Dispute Resolution** publishes a directory of over 450 community dispute resolution programs. For information, write to the Section at 740 Fifteenth Street, NW, Washington DC 20005-1009. You can also find out more information about the Section in the ABA's home page on the World Wide Web at http://www.abanet.org/dispute/home.html.
- **State bar associations** can provide information regarding lawyer referral services available in your state, and lawyer discipline and complaint procedures should you have a serious complaint about your attorney. Some states, including California, Florida, New Mexico, North Carolina, South Carolina, and Texas, certify lawyers in specialty areas such as estate planning.
- Your local **area agency on aging** should be able to inform you about the availability of free or reduced-fee legal assistance available to persons over sixty in your community. Look in your local government listings under "Aging" or call the **National**

Eldercare Locator at (800) 677-1116 to find the agency on aging nearest you. You can also search the database of the National Eldercare Locator on-line through their website at http://www.ageinfo.org/elderloc.

STATEWIDE LEGAL HOTLINES FOR THE ELDERLY IN OPERATION IN 1997

Arizona Hotline
Legal Hotline for the Elderly
Southern Arizona Legal Aid
Tucson
In-state: (800) 231-5441
Tucson and out-of-state: (602) 623-9465

Northern California Hotline
(serves only northern California counties)
Senior Legal Hotline
Legal Services of Northern California
Sacramento
In-state: (800) 222-1753
Sacramento and out-of-state: (916) 442-1212

District of Columbia Hotline
Legal Counsel for the Elderly
Washington, D.C.
(202) 434-2170

Florida Hotline
Legal Hotline for Older Floridians
Miami
(305) 576-5997

Hawaii Hotline
Senior Legal Hotline
Legal Aid Society of Hawaii
Honolulu
In-state: (800) 536-0011
Oahu and out-of-state: (808) 536-0011

Kansas Hotline
Legal Services of Wichita
Wichita
In-state: (888) 353-5337
Wichita and out-of-state: (316) 265-9681

Maine Hotline
Legal Hotline for the Elderly
Legal Services for the Elderly
Augusta
In-state: (800) 750-5353
Augusta and out-of-state: (207) 623-1797

Michigan Hotline
Legal Hotline for Older Michiganians
Lansing
In-state: (800) 347-5297
Lansing and out-of-state: (517) 372-5959

Mississippi Hotline
Statewide Elderly Hotline Service
South Mississippi Legal Services Corp.
Biloxi
In-state: (888) 660-0008
Out-of-state: (601) 374-4160

New Mexico Hotline
State Bar of New Mexico
Special Project, Inc., Lawyer Referral for the Elderly Program
Albuquerque
In-state: (800) 876-6657
Albuquerque and out-of-state: (505) 797-6005

Ohio Hotline
Legal Hotline for Ohioans
Pro Seniors, Inc.
Cincinnati
In-state: (800) 488-6070
Hamilton County and out-of-state: (513) 621-8721

Pennsylvania Hotline
Legal Hotline for Older Pennsylvanians
Pittsburgh
In-state: (800) 262-5297
Allegheny County and out-of-state: (412) 261-5297

Puerto Rico Hotline
Island-wide Seniors Legal Hotline
Puerto Rico Legal Services, Inc.
In-state: (800) 981-9160
Out-of-state: (787) 728-2323

Texas Hotline
Legal Hotline for Older Texans
Austin
In-state: (800) 622-2520
Travis County and out-of-state: (512) 477-3950

Health Care Advance Directive

CAUTION: This Health Care Advance Directive is a general form provided for your convenience. While it meets the legal requirements of most states, it may or may not fit the requirements or your particular state. Many states have special forms or special procedures for creating Health Care Advance Directives. If your state's law does not clearly recognize this document, it may still provide an effective statement of your wishes if you cannot speak for yourself. The directions for filling out the form are given first, followed by the form itself on page 227.

Section 1. Health Care Agent

Print your full name in this spot as the principal or creator of the health care advance directive.

Print the full name, address, and telephone number of the person (age eighteen or older) you appoint as your health care agent. Appoint *only* a person with whom you have talked and whom you trust to understand and carry out your values and wishes.

Many states limit the persons who can serve as your agent. If you want to meet all existing state restrictions, *do not* name any of the following as your agent, since some states will not let them act in that role:

This appendix is adapted from the booklet *Shape Your Health-Care Future with Health-Care Advance Directives*. The form may also be found on the ABA website: http://www.abnet.org/elderly.

- your health care providers, including physicians;
- staff of health care facilities or nursing care facilities providing your care;
- guardians of your finances (also called conservators);
- employees of government agencies financially responsible for your care;
- any person serving as agent for 10 or more persons.

Section 2. Alternate Agents

It is a good idea to name alternate agents in case your first agent is not available. Of course, only appoint alternates if you fully trust them to act faithfully as your agent and you have talked to them about serving as your agent. Print the appropriate information in this section. You can name as many alternate agents as you wish, but place them in the order you wish them to serve.

Section 3. Effective Date and Durability

This sample document is effective if and when you cannot make health care decisions. Your agent and your doctor determine if you are in this condition. Some state laws include specific procedures for determining your decision-making ability. If you wish, you can include other effective dates or other criteria for determining that you cannot make health care decisions (such as requiring two physicians to evaluate your decision-making ability). You also can state that the power will end at some later date or event before death.

In any case, you have the *right to revoke* or take away the agent's authority at any time. To revoke, notify your agent or health care provider orally or in writing. If you revoke, it is best to notify in writing both your agent and physician and anyone else who has a copy of the directive. Also destroy the health care advance directive document itself.

Section 4. Agent's Powers

This grant of power is intended to be as broad as possible. Unless you set limits, your agent will have authority to make any decision you could make to consent to or stop any type of health care.

Even under this broad grant of authority, your agent still must follow your wishes and directions, communicated by you in any manner now or in the future.

To specifically limit or direct your agent's power, you must complete Part II of the advance directive, section 6, on page 231.

Section 5. My Instructions About End-of-Life Treatment

The subject of end-of-life treatment is particularly important to many people. In this section, you can give general or specific instructions on the subject. The four main paragraphs are options—**choose only one**. Write your desires or instructions in your own words if you choose paragraph four. If you choose paragraph two, you have three additional options, from which you can choose one, two, or all three. If you are satisfied with your agent's knowledge of your values and wishes and you do not want to include instructions in the form, initial the first option and do not give instructions in the form.

Any instructions you give here will guide your agent. If you do not appoint an agent, they will guide any health care providers or surrogate decision-makers who must make a decision for you if you cannot do so yourself.

Directive in Your Own Words. If you would like to state your wishes about end-of-life treatment in your own words instead of choosing one of the options provided, you can do so in this section. Since people sometimes have different opinions on whether nutrition and hydration should be refused or stopped under certain circumstances, be sure to address this issue clearly in your directive. Nutrition and hydration means food and fluids given through a nasogastric tube or tube into your stomach, intestines, or veins, and *does not include* nonintrusive methods such as spoon feeding or moistening of lips and mouth.

Some states allow the stopping of nutrition and hydration only if you expressly authorize it. If you are creating your own directive, and you do not want nutrition and hydration, state so clearly.

Section 6. Any Other Health Care Instructions or Limitations or Modifications of my Agent's Powers

In this section, you can provide instructions about other health care issues that are not end-of-life treatment or nutrition and hydration. For example, you might want to include your wishes about issues such as nonemergency surgery, elective medical treatments, or admission to a nursing home. Again, be careful in these instructions not to place limitations on your agent that you do not intend. For example, while you may not want to be admitted to a nursing home, placing such a restriction may make things impossible for your agent if other options are not available.

You also may limit your agent's powers in any way you wish. For example, you can instruct your agent to refuse any specific types of treatment that are against your religious beliefs or unacceptable to you for any other reasons. These might include blood transfusions, electroconvulsive therapy, sterilization, abortion, amputation, psychosurgery, or admission to a mental institution, etc. Some states limit your agent's authority to consent to or refuse some of these procedures, regardless of your health care advance directive.

Be very careful about stating limitations, because the specific circumstances surrounding future health care decisions are impossible to predict. If you do not want any limitations, simply write in "*No limitations.*"

Section 7.
Protection of Third Parties Who Rely on My Agent

In most states, health care providers cannot be forced to follow the directions of your agent if they object. However most states also require providers to help transfer you to another provider who is willing to honor your instructions. To encourage compliance with the health care advance directive, this paragraph states that providers who rely in good faith on the agent's statements and decisions will not be held civilly liable for their actions.

Section 8. Donations of Organs at Death

In this section you can state your intention to donate bodily organs and tissues at death. If you do not wish to be an organ donor, initial the first option. The second option is a donation of any or all organs or parts. The third option allows you to donate only those organs or tissues you specify. Consider mentioning the heart, liver, lung, kidney, pancreas, intestine, cornea, bone, skin, heart valves, tendons, ligaments, and saphenous vein. Finally, you may limit the use of your organs by *crossing out* any of the four purposes listed that you do not want (transplant, research, therapy, or education). If you do not cross out any of these options, your organs may be used for any of these purposes.

Section 9. Nomination of Guardian

Appointing a health care agent helps to avoid a court-appointed guardian for health care decision-making. However, if a court becomes involved for any reason, this paragraph expressly names your agent to serve as guardian. A court does not have to follow your nomination, but normally it will honor your wishes unless there is good reason to override your choice.

Section 10. Administrative Provisions

These items address miscellaneous matters that could affect the implementation of your health care advance directive.

Signing the Document

Required state procedures for signing this kind of document vary. Some require only a signature, while others have very detailed witnessing requirements. Some states simply require notarization.

The procedure in this book is likely to be far more complex than your state law requires because it combines the formal requirements from virtually every state. Follow it if you do not know your state's requirements and you want to meet the signature requirements of virtually every state.

First, sign and date the document in the presence of two witnesses and a notary. Your witnesses should know your identity personally and be able to declare that you appear to be of sound mind and under no duress or undue influence.

In order to meet the different witnessing requirements of most states, do *not* have the following people witness your signature:

- Anyone you have chosen to make health care decisions on your behalf (agent or alternate agents).
- Your treating physician, health care provider, health facility operator, or an employee of any of these.
- Insurers or employees of your life/health insurance provider.
- Anyone financially responsible for your health care costs.
- Anyone related to you by blood, marriage, or adoption.
- Anyone entitled to any part of your estate under an existing will or by operation of law or anyone who will benefit financially from your death. Your creditors should not serve as witnesses.

If you are in a nursing home or other institution, a few states have additional witnessing requirements. This form does not include witnessing language for this situation. Contact a patient advocate or an ombudsman to find out about the state's requirements in these cases.

Second, have your signature notarized. Some states permit notarization as an alternative to witnessing. Doing both witnessing and notarization is more than most states require, but doing both will meet the execution requirements of most states. This form includes a typical notary statement, but it is wise to check state law in case it requires a special form of notary acknowledgment.

HEALTH CARE ADVANCE DIRECTIVE

PART I
APPOINTMENT OF HEALTH CARE AGENT

1. HEALTH CARE AGENT

I, ______________________________________, hereby appoint
PRINCIPAL

____
AGENT'S NAME

____
ADDRESS

________________________ ________________________
HOME PHONE # WORK PHONE #

as my agent to make health and personal care decisions for me as authorized in this document.

2. ALTERNATE AGENTS

If

- I revoke my Agent's authority; or
- my Agent becomes unwilling or unavailable to act; or
- my agent is my spouse and I become legally separated or divorced,

I name the following (each to act alone and successively, in the order named) as alternates to my Agent:

A. First Alternate Agent ______________________________

Address ______________________________________

Telephone ______________________________

B. Second Alternate Agent ______________________

Address ______________________________

Telephone ______________________________

3. EFFECTIVE DATE AND DURABILITY

By this document I intend to create a health care advance directive. It is effective upon, and only during, any period in which I cannot make or communicate a choice regarding a particular health care decision. My Agent, attending physician, and any other necessary experts should determine that I am unable to make choices about health care.

4. AGENT'S POWERS

I give my Agent full authority to make health care decisions for me. My Agent shall follow my wishes as known to my Agent either through this document or through other means. In interpreting my wishes, I intend my Agent's authority to be as broad as possible, except for any limitations I state in this form. In making any decision, my Agent shall try to discuss the proposed decision with me to determine my desires if I am able to communicate in any way. If my Agent cannot determine the choice I would want, then my Agent shall make a choice for me based upon what my Agent believes to be in my best interests.

Unless specifically limited by Section 6, below, my Agent is authorized as follows:

A. To consent, refuse, or withdraw consent to any and all types of health care. Health care means any care, treatment, service, or procedure to maintain, diagnose, or otherwise affect an individual's physical or mental condition. It includes, but is not limited to, artificial respiration, nutritional support and hydration, medication, and cardiopulmonary resuscitation;

B. To have access to medical records and information to the same extent that I am entitled, including the right to disclose the contents to others as appropriate for my health care;

C. To authorize my admission to or discharge from (even against medical advice) any hospital, nursing home, residential care, assisted living facility, or similar facility or service;

D. To contract on my behalf for any health care related service or facility on my behalf, without my Agent incurring personal financial liability for such contracts;

E. To hire and fire medical, social service, and other support personnel responsible for my care;

F. To authorize, or refuse to authorize, any medication or procedure intended to relieve pain, even though such use may lead to physical damage or addiction or hasten the moment of (but not intentionally cause) my death;

G. To make anatomical gifts of part or all of my body for medical purposes, authorize an autopsy, and direct the disposition of my remains, to the extent permitted by law;

H. To take any other action necessary to do what I authorize here, including (but not limited to) granting any waiver or release from liability required by any hospital, physician, or other health care provider; signing any documents relating to refusals of treatment or the leaving of a facility against medical advice; and pursuing any legal action in my name at the expense of my estate to force compliance with my wishes as determined by my Agent, or to seek actual or punitive damages for the failure to comply.

PART II
INSTRUCTIONS ABOUT HEALTH CARE

5. MY INSTRUCTIONS ABOUT END-OF-LIFE TREATMENT

(INITIAL ONLY ONE OF THE FOLLOWING FOUR MAIN STATEMENTS):

1. _____ **NO SPECIFIC INSTRUCTIONS.** My Agent knows my values and wishes, so I do not wish to include any specific instructions here.

2. _____ **DIRECTIVE TO WITHHOLD OR WITHDRAW TREATMENT.** Although I greatly value life, I also believe that at some point life has such diminished value that medical treatment should be stopped, and I should be allowed to die. Therefore, I do not want to receive treatment, including nutrition and hydration, when the treatment will not give me a meaningful quality of life.
   (IF YOU INITIALED THIS PARAGRAPH, ALSO INITIAL ANY OR ALL OF THE FOLLOWING THREE STATEMENTS WITH WHICH YOU AGREE):
   By this I mean that I do not want my life prolonged . . .
   _____ . . . if the treatment will leave me in a condition of permanent unconsciousness, such as in an irreversible coma or a persistent vegetative state.
   _____ . . . if the treatment will leave me with no more than some consciousness and in an irreversible condition of complete, or nearly complete, loss of ability to think or communicate with others.
   _____ . . . if the treatment will leave me with no more than some ability to think or communicate with others, and the likely risks and burdens of treatment outweigh the expected benefits. Risks, burdens, and benefits include consideration of length of life, quality of life, financial costs, and my personal dignity and privacy.

3. _____ **DIRECTIVE TO RECEIVE TREATMENT.** I want my life to be prolonged as long as possible, no matter what my quality of life.

4. _____ **DIRECTIVE ABOUT END-OF-LIFE TREATMENT IN MY OWN WORDS:**

____

____

____

____

____

6. ANY OTHER HEALTH CARE INSTRUCTIONS OR LIMITATIONS OR MODIFICATIONS OF MY AGENT'S POWERS

____

____

____

____

____

7. PROTECTION OF THIRD PARTIES WHO RELY ON MY AGENT

No person who relies in good faith upon any representations by my Agent or Alternate Agent(s) shall be liable to me, my estate, or my heirs or assigns, for recognizing the Agent's authority.

8. DONATIONS OF ORGANS AT DEATH

Upon my death:
(Initial one)

_____ I do *not* wish to donate any organs or tissues, OR

_____ I give *any* needed organs, tissues, or parts, OR

_____ I give *only* the following organs, tissues, or parts:

(please specify)

____

____

____

My gift (if any) is for the following purposes:
(Cross out any of the following you do not want)

- Transplant
- Research

- Therapy
- Education

9. NOMINATION OF GUARDIAN

If a guardian of my person should for any reason need to be appointed, I nominate my Agent (or his or her alternate then authorized to act), named above.

10. ADMINISTRATIVE PROVISIONS

(All apply)

- I revoke any prior health care advance directive.
- This health care advance directive is intended to be valid in any jurisdiction in which it is presented.
- A copy of this advance directive is intended to have the same effect as the original.

SIGNING THE DOCUMENT

BY SIGNING HERE I INDICATE THAT I UNDERSTAND THE CONTENTS OF THIS DOCUMENT AND THE EFFECT OF THIS GRANT OF POWERS TO MY AGENT.

I sign my name to this Health Care Advance Directive on this

______day of _________________________, 19_____.

My Signature ____________________________________

My Name _______________________________________

My current home address is _________________________

____

____

WITNESS STATEMENT

I declare that the person who signed or acknowledged this document is personally known to me, that he/she signed or acknowledged this health care advance directive in my presence, and that he/she appears to be of sound mind and under no duress, fraud, or undue influence.

I am not:

- the person appointed as agent by this document;
- the patient's health care provider;
- an employee of the patient's health care provider;
- financially responsible for the person's health care;
- related to the principal by blood, marriage, or adoption; and,
- to the best of my knowledge, a creditor of the principal or entitled to any part of his/her estate under a will now existing or by operation of law.

Witness #1:

____

SIGNATURE DATE

____

PRINT NAME

____

RESIDENT ADDRESS

____

TELEPHONE

Witness #2:

____

SIGNATURE DATE

____

PRINT NAME

____

RESIDENT ADDRESS

____

TELEPHONE

Notarization

STATE OF ________________.) My Commission Expires:

) ss.

COUNTY OF __________________.)

On this _____ day of ___________, 19_____,

the said ________________________, known to me (or satisfactorily proven) to be the person named in the foregoing instrument, personally appeared before me, a Notary Public, within and for the State and County aforesaid, and acknowledged that he or she freely and voluntarily executed the same for the purposes stated therein.

____

NOTARY PUBLIC

INDEX

ABOUT THE AUTHORS

CHARLES P. SABATINO is the assistant director of the American Bar Association's Commission on Legal Problems of the Elderly. Since 1984, he has been responsible for commission research, project development, and education in areas of health law, long-term care, decision making, and legal services delivery for the elderly, including professional ethics. He is a part-time adjunct professor at Georgetown University Law Center, where he teaches Law and Aging, and he is a fellow and board member of the National Academy of Elder Law Attorneys.

The ABA Commission staff co-authors are STEPHANIE EDELSTEIN; NAOMI KARP; LORI STIEGEL; ERICA WOOD; and NANCY COLEMAN, director. The Commission on Legal Problems of the Elderly is dedicated to examining the law-related concerns of older persons. Established by the American Bar Association in 1978, the commission has sought to improve legal services for the elderly, has explored a wide range of legal and policy issues, and provides over ninety publications and videos to professionals and the public, including the quarterly newsletter *Bifocal*.

6556